CRYSTAL CLEAR
ORACLE

Loving Guidance from
the Mineral Kingdom

NADINE GORDON-TAYLOR

Bear & Company
Rochester, Vermont

Bear & Company
One Park Street
Rochester, Vermont 05767
www.BearandCompanyBooks.com

Bear & Company is a division of Inner Traditions International

ISBN 978-1-59143-484-9 (print)

Printed and bound in China by Reliance Printing Co., Ltd.

10   9   8   7   6   5   4   3   2   1

Text design and layout by Virginia Scott Bowman
This book was typeset in Garamond Premier Pro with Gill Sans Nova used as the display
typeface
Artwork by Nadine Gordon-Taylor

To send correspondence to the author of this book, mail a first-class letter to the author
c/o Inner Traditions • Bear & Company, One Park Street, Rochester, VT 05767, and we
will forward the communication, or contact the author directly at **ngtartist@optonline
.net**, or visit her website, **thethirdeyestudio.com**.

I dedicate this to all the beautiful and sensitive crystals who have been with me since childhood—and to all the crystals included in this book who guided me with their wise words.

CONTENTS

ACKNOWLEDGMENTS

What an honor it is to have Inner Traditions/Bear & Company publish my third oracle deck. I am so grateful for their unwavering support.

I wish to acknowledge my indebtedness and gratitude to all those who helped in the preparation of the Crystal Clear Oracle Cards. My heartfelt thanks go out to the following for their invaluable help:

Doris Renza—For her love, friendship, humor, and design acumen.

Mark Sarazen—For years and years of amazing technological support.

Ted Taylor—For his clever and brilliant relationship with words and help with anything grammatical.

And to my daughter, Masha, who like an angel, watched over the entire project, blessing it with her intuition and wisdom.

A MESSAGE FROM
THE ARTIST/AUTHOR

A shamanic practitioner I once knew handed me a very large, heavy quartz crystal and left the room to do something. I held it in my arms, admiring its beauty, and within seconds, a male form rose out of it like a hologram. I was alarmed at first—then astonished—and then fascinated. He did not say anything, but I could see him moving about with my third eye. When my friend came back, I mentioned to her that there was a man in the crystal. She laughed and responded nonchalantly that she knew and was curious to see if I could sense it too. She was impressed and said it was programmed with information a long time ago. I always felt a connection with stones, but this was an aha moment for me. When I studied geology in school, I was never taught that stones could be programmed.

My fascination with stones started when I was a child. I grew up in a household where stones were everywhere: fossils my brother dug up; fine crystal jewelry from around the world; and beautiful, unusual specimens were scattered in every room of the house. I never knew all their names, but I sensed their beautiful energy. My older brother studied geology and paleobotany, and my father was (among other things) a lapidary jeweler. Weekends would be spent digging at the Delaware Water Gap or visiting rock and mineral shows. Family vacations would take place at national parks, where my brother and I would discuss the unique rock formations. I think he was in college when he got a job working in an amethyst mine in South West Africa, now Namibia (from which I benefited immensely—I still have some of the beautiful specimens he sent me). My brother's love of working with stones was contagious, and soon my dad took over his saw, grinder, and polisher. To my mother's dismay, you could always find him in the basement (after work and on weekends) creating his masterpieces. He was prolific. He would create the most beautiful rings, pendants, and earrings and use my mother and me as models to show them off to friends and family. He was so admired for his creative settings that a Madison Avenue crystal gallery invited him to show his work. I am still surrounded by large pieces of sodalite, tiger's eye, and obsidian, to name a few, that he started cutting and never finished.

Crystals and humans have collaborated since prehistoric times. They have been used for tools, adornment, as protection in shields, as advice for oracles, and in religious ceremonies for connecting with higher powers. They have been worshipped, collected, studied, categorized, and valued. Over the centuries their healing information and metaphysical powers were passed down until the present day where they are more popular than ever before. It's time for a new perspective. Everything we have ever learned about life on this planet is about to change. We are at the threshold of a new consciousness, a new way of existing. Unlike what is written in science books, Earth (Gaia) is more than a spherical rock turning in a vast cosmos. It is a conscious being and its stones and crystals are very much alive. Their energy just vibrates at a slower frequency than other life-forms. Funny enough, my first experience with this type of information came from science fiction. I have been a Trekkie since elementary school and watched a 1967 episode from the original *Star Trek* series called "The Devil in the Dark." The crew of the *Enterprise,* being ignorant and headstrong, had destroyed the eggs of a silicon-based species that lived in and fed on rocks. It was a mother Horta—and it fought back to save her children. It was of course a miscommunication and all was resolved in the end with a mind-meld from Spock. It was strange to think that rocks had feelings. But what resonated with me about the moral of the story was that man and rock worked together for the betterment of each other and the planet. One doesn't have to be Vulcan or a shaman to connect with crystals. You can communicate with them too. The more you work with them, the more sensitive you become. Whether you hold an actual crystal in your hands or view an image of it, you connect with its intelligence. Start by giving it attention. Close your eyes, touch its surface, and breath slowly. Soon you will experience your own "mind-meld."

Humans have turned to divination for guidance and answers since biblical times and probably before. Divination is a way to give order to what seems like a random, chaotic, and at times perilous existence. In some ways, it also gives comfort knowing there is something much bigger than ourselves out there. To our ancient ancestors believing in the gods was like having attentive parents who had all the answers and would be there in times of need. I believe we do have access to something special—call it Gaia, God, Higher Self, Guardian Angels, Soul Guides, Source, or even Quantum Physics. I have been called by the stones to share my experiences and talents with you. The Crystal Clear Oracle Cards have been created to acknowledge the inspiring wisdom and healing advice from Gaia's children—her rocks, stones, and crystals. These cards provide you with an open channel to your personal intuitive portal—one that connects your heart with your Higher Self. It activates and aligns you with what you need to hear to help you move forward on your journey. It is about allowing emotional and spiritual wisdom into your life and being ready to let this maturation process work its magic. When used regularly, the cards act as a catalyst, nudging you to wake up and see things as they are, not as you think they are. You learn that your actions create your reality. You steer the ship and decide which course to take.

The constructive and positive messages found in this book allow you to access new and loving energies that inspire, empower, and heal. These messages come directly from the crystals that appear in each image. They act as guides explaining their qualities, attributes, and properties and then assist you in understanding and decoding the other symbols that have accompanied them. The stones included in this deck contacted me—not the other way around. They have manifested here because they want their voices to be heard. When you select cards from this deck, you summon their energy and very much need to hear what they have to say. Trust that process; it is always correct. Remember, you are always held in the heart of Divine love when you work with the Crystal Clear Oracle Cards.

Blessings from my heart to yours.

Nadine Gordon-Taylor

HOW TO USE THE CRYSTAL CLEAR ORACLE CARDS

Working with divination cards is a very personal thing. I believe there is no one correct way to use them. Over time, you will cultivate certain preferences. It's really more about how much time you have and if you are doing the reading for yourself or others. I would advise trying out different spreads; this allows your Higher Self more varied opportunities to communicate with you. In the end, though, you always, and I repeat, *always,* attract the card with the message you most need to hear. This point is exemplified by the following stories: A couple visited my gallery after seeing an original painting of mine hanging in the café next door. The woman really admired the image; it seemed to resonate with the new business she had just started. Well, unbeknown to her, her husband was planning on buying it for her but hadn't told her yet. She saw my oracle cards on the table and got very excited and asked if she could pull one. I handed her the deck and she shuffled. While shuffling, a card flew up into the air and fell to the floor—and it was a card with the image of the painting he wanted to buy her. Another time, a young man came into my gallery looking for a present for his brother. He was not particularly into New Age art but came in anyway. I showed him my *Animal Love* deck and when I opened the box for him, I'm not sure why, but the cow card was on top facing up. He seemed surprised. He said his brother was a farmer and loved cows. He ended up buying him a cow print.

As special as these synchronistic stories seem, they are quite common. Using the Crystal Clear Oracle Cards is all about strengthening your intuition. You (and your intuition) are directly connected to Source (God, matrix, etc.). When you focus on a question and ask Source for guidance, it energetically attracts to you that which you need to hear. This deck will help you if you are ready to let go of past beliefs and embrace the wonderful new energies that we can all access.

The following are some suggestions when working with the Crystal Clear Oracle Cards (or any cards), but please feel free to listen to your own muse and try out new methods. No matter what you do or don't do, you will always receive a powerful message—just allow it in . . . and have fun!

Getting Started: Balancing Your Deck and Creating an Uplifting Space

The following list can get you in the mood and declare to the universe that you are ready to receive. Depending on the situation, I like to do some of the following suggestions some of the time because that is how I learned (and I feel they are important), but I have never noticed any difference in the results of the readings if I spontaneously pick up a deck and use it. And when I give readings at fairs and work with many people one right after the other, I have always had amazing results no matter what I did or didn't do. I state an intention knowing any readings I give will be helpful—and so they are. Since everything you create starts with a belief system, a thought, it is up to you whether these or any other rituals are important. Pick any of the following suggestions that resonate with you.

Connecting with Source
I recommend whenever you work with cards, channelers, or doing energy healing on others, picture an energetic cord going through your spine up through the crown chakra and extending to the Source or God. At the same time, see one going down your spine

through your base chakra, grounding yourself to the Earth. This way, you understand it is Source doing the mental, physical, and spiritual healing work and not you. You are just the vehicle that allows it to happen. And you will stay safe. Energy will pass through you but not affect you.

Knocking on the Deck Three Times

Some practitioners knock on their decks three times before giving a reading. This practice seems to be related to the phrase "knock on wood" that dates back to ancient folklore when people believed spirits lived in trees. Touching the wood would invoke protection and/or blessings from the spirits within. Cards are made from paper that comes from trees, so I can see the connection. Some also believe tapping removes old energy, allowing a fresh start.

Blowing

You can spread your cards down on a surface or just fan them out in your hand and blow on them. Feel and see your breath coming directly from Source.

Envisioning a Clear Mind

It is best to work when you don't have any distractions—it allows energy to flow, but it also allows you to be a better receiver as well. You can clear your mind with positive affirmations such as:

I lovingly clear any extraneous and unnecessary thoughts from my mind and send them back where they came from.
My focus is razor sharp and I easily tap into the universal mind of Source.

Or more simply put:

My mind is clear and open to receiving.

Meditating

When you relax your mind, distractions from your day fade away and you become a more neutral receiver. All you need to do is focus on your breathing and your body will do the rest. I have found that "Square Breathing" is very good to slow everything down—it even lowers your blood pressure (I have actually documented that with a blood pressure cuff). To do Square Breathing, breathe in for the count of four, hold for the count of four, exhale to the count of four. Do this four times. At the same time, you can play soft, relaxing music to help you shift your brain frequencies—if you like.

Fragrances

Burning incense or spraying your space and/or deck with sage spray is a lovely way to clear your space and cards. It sets a special mood, letting you know it's time to relax. You can pick your favorite aromatherapy—the many essential oils affect you in different ways. It is a subtle effect, but powerful. If you want an extreme clearing of the cards, you can light a piece of sage and expose each card to the smoke. Not only does it cleanse the cards, but many ancient cultures believed the smoke was sacred and opened up a conduit to the spirit world.

Bay Leaves

These aromatic laurel leaves are known to increase psychic abilities. They are also associated with victory, protection, healing, success, and love. You can keep your cards wrapped in them at any time—or if you know you're doing a reading for someone, wrap them the night before.

Sound

If you are fortunate enough to have a set of singing bowls, select the size (and chakra) you want to use and place the cards near or directly inside the bowl. Let the sound permeate both you and the cards. Singing bowls are known to promote relaxation and have powerful healing properties, but they are not the only healing sound to choose from. Steel tongue drums made from propane tanks offer powerful and enchanting sounds and change the vibrations of your space. You can put your cards inside the hollow opening in the bottom to drench them with these angelic sounds. Table chimes and bells are also gentle ways to shift energy. If you have no musical instruments, you may use your own soft humming voice or even chant over them.

Crystals
Select any *protective* crystals (black stones are usually known for this) and place them on top of the deck overnight before any reading. It is a good idea to keep them close by when reading as well. The more protection the better! You can also pick a stone by its beauty or just your intuition. They each individually can help in different ways.

Charging the Cards
When you have finished any of the above rituals (and even when you haven't done anything special), I always recommend taking your cards in your hands and holding them to your heart. This is the best and quickest way to become a loving, positive, divine conduit.

Let's Go: Questions, Shuffling, and Reversals

There are a variety of card spreads that you can select from—or you can invent your own—but whichever one you choose, it's traditional to shuffle the cards and ask your question. I suggest you leave your questions open-ended to bring in all possibilities. If you do get specific, you need to interpret the question in a slightly different way to understand the message. For example, if you ask about something going on in a relationship and you pull a card with a dog in it, this could mean that the person in question is indeed being faithful to you, or it could mean that you need to be more faithful to them. Also, I would avoid "should" questions. I don't seem to get answers when I do this. Some examples of questions to ask:

What is it that I need most to know at this time?
What needs to be revealed for my soul's growth?

Or if you want to get a bit more specific—

What do I need to know for my healing?
What is the energy or truth around my job (health, relationship, or any other situation)?

Of course, you don't need to ask any questions at all. Your Higher Self, or what I call Divine Love, will always have your back. Whatever message you receive will always be what you need to hear. When selecting a card or cards I sometimes move my hands over them until I feel a connection. You can also shuffle until one jumps out. Listen to your intuition. You will be guided. I tend to read the cards from my decks right side up because there is so much information in them. But if a card is reversed, it does not mean it is negative. It could be that you need to hear more about the particular lesson you are going through.

The painted images in this deck are quite intricate. My first deck was small, and the users of that deck suggested a larger format. That is why the cards in this deck measure 4 × 5.75 inches (and not the standard 2.75 × 4.75 inches). Although this can make the common horizontal overhand shuffle challenging for some, if you turn the cards vertically, it makes it easier to do. The same is true with the riffle and bridge or dovetail shuffles.

Choosing and Interpreting Your Card Spreads

Single Card Spread

Card spreads are fun but can get quite complicated and time-consuming. I recommend the single card pull whenever you want to get the most direct message for yourself or someone you are reading for in the shortest amount of time. Pull a card every day if you want to exercise your intuitive muscle, so to speak. You can read the words printed on the card and/or listen to what thoughts come into your mind. For example, below is the Moonstone card with the words *Change, Mystery, and Balancing Cycles.* The first thought I had was that the bear is standing tall. Next, you can reflect in a journal and explore what standing tall means for you. Work with the energy of this expression and create an affirmation or affirmations. For example,

When I go with the flow and acknowledge the mysteries and cycles of life, I know I can handle anything.

Or more simply stated,

I am proud and confident of who I am.

When you are finished with this exercise, you can then read the message in the guidebook to enhance your experience. The more you do this process, the better you get.

Moonstone
Change, Mystery, and Balancing Cycles

Three Card or Four Card Spread

When you feel you understand how to read one card and want a more in-depth understanding, you can pull three cards. This spread is one of the most popular and represents the Past, Present, and Future. The first card would interpret what brought you to where you are now (the past), the middle card would share your current issues (the present), and the card to the right of that will give you a glimpse of your next lesson (the future). You can pull a fourth card to continue the reading, adding it like a clarifier or Outcome card providing more information. This spread needs to be given adequate time for you to meditate on each card and understand the main lessons you feel you either have learned or need to learn. It would be good to keep a journal of your readings for a while to see your intellectual and spiritual progression. As with the single card, you can use the words printed on each card, or select your own. The following is an example of words that came to me when using the Ruby, Tiger's Eye, Jasper, and Aquamarine cards.

Past	Present	Future	Outcome

Ruby	Tiger's Eye	Jasper	Aquamarine
Past	Present	Future	Outcome
Evolution/Growth	Patient/Boundaries	Family/Love	Connection/Fun

From these cards came the following affirmations:

I learn loving lessons from my family and have fun as I grow.
I am continually evolving and am patient with the process.
I set appropriate boundaries with friends and family.
My loving family is there for me; we are always connected and having fun together.

You can also explore the cards separately and ask questions:

How am I evolving and changing? What growth did I see in the past?
Do I need to develop more patience in my life? Where?
Am I able to unconditionally love my family?
Do I feel connected and have fun with my friends? If yes, how? If not, why not?

And just keep going with whatever questions and insights surface. The guidebook is here to enrich the experience and can be read before or after journaling—it's your choice.

Tarot
Any spreads you find in tarot books like the Celtic Cross would work with the Crystal Clear Oracle Cards as well. They are more complex and time-consuming, but often just what is needed.

Face Up
One last suggestion I have is holding the deck in your hands or spreading them out on a table with the front facing you. Go through each card until you find one you fixate on—you can't take your eyes off of it. This card wants to speak with you! Work with it.

Create Your Own
I want to encourage you to make up your own layouts—look to different cultures (like Celtic, Native American, etc.) or nature for

inspiration. For example, set your cards out like a tree, starting with one or two cards at the bottom for the past and branching out toward the future as you move up. You can also use the cardinal directions. Be inventive and creative. Your imagination is the limit! And after doing a reading, take note of how you feel emotionally, spiritually, and physically. With these new insights, you might want to create something wonderful. Write, draw, paint, collage, compose, dance, and/or sing.

A Little Something Extra

Clarifying Cards/Pendulum

If you want more information about a particular card or spread in general, you can add an extra card(s) to help you uncover even more information about your situation. This card can be from the same deck or an entirely different one. You can also swing a pendulum over the spread or a specific card, asking helpful questions.

Crystals

I encourage you to add crystals to any layout. Use your intuition and select stones that call to you. They have a gentle energy, bringing poignant insights to any interpretation. If you have a crystal collection, you can use it with the card pull. Lay the stone directly on the card or hold it in your hands and read the message.

Process Journal

This intimate sketchbook is unlike most—it is an idea diary, a tool that documents your journey into the creative spirit, allowing conscious and unconscious imagery to emerge. It is a hybrid art and writing book—a place to create without any restrictions. It is called a process journal because it is always evolving, in process—never finished. There is no right or wrong, good or bad—just the act of creating. You can continuously alter it adding more layers over time, working and reworking pages. It is a place to explore your thoughts using traditional and nontraditional materials and methods. You can:

Draw
Paint
Stamp
Use makeup
Use pastels
Use watercolors
Use acrylics
Use colored pencils
Use drawing pencils
Use charcoal pencils
Alter the shapes of pages
Cut out sections of the page
Add things to existing pages

Attach more paper with tabs
Weave in different papers
Collage
Write by hand or add print-
    outs with text
Erase images
Tie things in
Staple images in
Use photographs
Be realistic
Be abstract
Be nonobjective

Process journals work well with themes such as documenting your daily synchronicities and dreams or illustrating the story of your soul growth (perhaps through the messages you receive from the Crystal Clear Oracle Cards). Pull a card every day and examine it closely. Create a one or two page spread. Photograph the card and print it out—or draw it. Look at all the symbols in the card and investigate each one in depth. Explore everything your mind can think of in terms of pictures, songs, quotations, prose, poetry, blogs, or doodling. The possibilities are endless. These personal records often become works of art in their own right and are special keepsakes.

Affirmations

At the end of each crystal message are three affirmations designed to trigger reflective insights. The number three was chosen because it resonates with the energies of creation and completion. These affirmations are positive thoughts in the present tense focusing on abundance, prosperity, growth, and peace. I have included them to help you concentrate on what is important—reaching your goals, building your confidence, reminding you how powerful you are, and finding love (personal and universal). Repetition is key. Use these affirmations on a daily basis to help you break free from any limiting thoughts and patterns. The more often you read them silently to yourself or speak them out loud, the more you integrate them into your consciousness and shift not only your mood but your current timeline.

Glossary

I have included a list of words and terms in the glossary section at the end of the book that I believe could use further clarification. I include them to enhance your experience of using the cards. I feel it is more appropriate to explain them in depth in the glossary than in the messages. If you don't understand a word or concept and you would like to know how I define it, just check at the back of the guidebook.

Divination cards are just an extension of yourself.

Remember to work with the cards with
a light heart and a sense of joy.

Let the child in you come out and play—
in the heart of the Universe.

ALEXANDRITE
The Discriminating Manifestor
Abundance, Joy, and Self-Confidence

I am Alexandrite, a rare form of chrysoberyl, and I see how special you are. I have chameleonlike qualities. I am known as "emerald by day, and ruby by night." This is because I appear as a lovely green in daylight, and a purplish red in incandescent light. In this image, it is fitting that I appear at the head of the energetic figurative portal since I am a stone of the intellect and associated with the crown chakra. You have chosen this card because you would like to bring prosperity, balance, and good fortune into your life. I can help you do that by sharing my wisdom. The most important thing I can teach you is that you create reality with your mind. There is an expression: if you want to know what you were thinking five years ago, look at your life today, and if you want to know what your life will look like in five years, look at your thoughts today. So be very discerning with what you believe, think, and speak. Some of your ideas are based on misconceptions. One example is that you feel you are alone. You are not. I want to introduce you to the most important person in your life—you! Gaze into the mirror and meet yourself; you two are a perfect match and will be together for a long time. You will heal and have fun together. You don't have to look outside yourself for anything anymore. You have learned your lessons from the past and can put them behind you forever. Wear me on your finger (I make an excellent engagement ring) or around your neck, and feel my loving, kind, joyful, optimistic, forgiving, cooperative, and considerate energy surround you. Ask me if I want to live in the present moment together with you—I do!

Joining our journey are a clouded leopard, two pink roses, twenty kelp pearls, two blue perches, Saturn, and four portals. The portals lead to alternate timelines and dimensions. Teleport through these "stargates" and remove all that is blocking your memory. You discover the real you when you peel back the layers of imprinting that you have collected from all your past lives, emotional journeys, and traumatic experiences. How nice for you to meet yourself for the first time. Listen to your Higher Self and focus your thoughts and attention on completing any creative projects you started in the past—they are more important than you realize. Live your life with courage, integrity, and unconditional love, and be a positive example for others to follow.

Remember that things might seem a bit tangled right now (because of Saturn), but all lessons will sort themselves out over time. The twenty kelp pearls offer protection and a safe spiritual home for the blue perches (creativity and abundance) to rejuvenate after a long day. Let go of anything that keeps you from seeing the beauty and love in your life. All emotions, ideas, information, and beliefs exist simultaneously in the morphic field. You are an antenna. What energy and signals are you going to attract and listen to? Peace, abundance, and happiness are floating all around you—just tune in to them and receive your blessings. The two pink roses want you to admire yourself and all you have achieved, no matter how small. When you share one of these roses with someone special, you open up a portal of love and meet others on the same frequency. The clouded leopard wants you to know that the truth about this reality has been hidden from you—it has been camouflaged. But, if you look hard enough, you will recognize its energetic signature and see it for what it actually is. Allow the clouded leopard and me, Alexandrite, to ground you, knowing you will always land on your feet.

Affirmations

I love myself more today than yesterday.

I am my own best friend and don't need validation from others.

I have as many loving relationships as there are stars in the universe.

AMBER
The Courageous Chronicler
Empowerment, Healing, and Letting Go

I am Amber, an ancient fossilized tree resin, and I can heal your wounds. Although my name means "brownish yellow," I also come in golden, white, orange, and even bluish-green colors. I am not really a stone, but I am still considered a valuable gem. In this image, you see me balancing on the head of a pigeon. You have chosen this card because you want to release old, negative programming. I know how to do that. I have been around a long time (about 320 million years) and have seen and learned much. I can show you how to set appropriate boundaries, helping you to stay composed no matter what infiltrates your sphere. Think of me as a Band-Aid that forms a protective, healing seal around your body, mind, and soul. If you hold or wear a piece of me, you will find that the limiting, critical voice you sometimes hear will dissipate, and a gentle, new, patient one will take its place. My cleansing and renewing energy will also help remove things that cause mental and emotional stress, allowing you to feel more stable, empowered, and ready to tackle your soul purpose.

Joining our journey are a pink-necked green pigeon, a buckeye butterfly, a giant snail, a pinecone, two trees, Jupiter, three balloon flowers, and a damselfly. The damselfly lived and died about 30–90 million years ago! She is telling you to see old, unresolved situations from a new perspective and resolve them now. One way is to make sure you speak with beautiful vibrations like the cooing of the pigeon. Listen to your voice—is it filled with love? Are you adding unconditional love to the universal web? The present timeline can be altered with your sounds. You must realize that your activities, emotions, and beliefs go into creating reality on this planet. Anchor yourself in high-frequency energies because they automatically connect you to everyone, everywhere (quantum entanglement).

Like the snail, you need to come out of your shell and keep your feet on the ground. It says if you take your time and are mindful, you will achieve your dreams. Jupiter and the buckeye butterfly see that you are larger and more influential than you realize. They believe your intuition will help you achieve greatness in ways you don't even understand yet—no matter how old you are! The balloon flowers and buds remind you that you are always transforming. Never think for a moment that you know who you are since you slowly evolve and change all the time. This is echoed in the snail's spiral shell as well. Heraclitus (the Greek philosopher) clearly understood this when he said, "No man ever steps in the same river twice, for it's not the same river, and he's not the same man." These ancient pine trees are deeply rooted in the Earth and grow from divine, cosmic love. The heart on the pigeon's breast, the shape of the amber, and the heart-shaped portal vibrate with love. They are here to show you that you can be involved in close relationships—if you want. Don't be afraid of loving too much. On top sits the wise pinecone, radiating enlightenment. It says that when you believe in and use your *third eye,* you will bypass the limitations of the brain and land directly in the eternal heart. Remember to summon me, Amber, when you need the courage and self-confidence to grow and thrive here in your galactic home.

Affirmations

As I grow in awareness, I am renewed and energized.

I set appropriate and loving boundaries that help others as much as myself.

I am a part of the Earth and the Earth is a part of me; what happens to her, happens to me.

AMETHYST
The Eternal Caregiver
Peace, Protection, and Compassionate Purification

I am Amethyst, a form of purple quartz that forms on the inner surface of a geode, and I understand you. I come in many variations of purple: pale rose, lilac with pink undertones, coolish blue, and a reddish variety known as "raspberry." I am a hard stone and can be cut and faceted into almost any shape you like. In this image, my heart-shaped crystal is being held up in front of the waterfall. You have chosen this card because you want to be mentally, emotionally, and spiritually balanced. I can help you with that. My name comes from the Greek word *amethystos,* meaning "not intoxicated." You may have developed some habits that you want to change. Well, I am here to activate your third eye and help you reduce any anxiety and addictions. Place me on your forehead and/or heart, and I will absorb any negativity with my calm and tranquil nature. This enables me to act as a protective shield.

Joining our journey are the Egyptian god Horus, waterworkers, a goldfish, the Full Moon, three tortoises, ants, and a waterfall. Horus has stepped through the (time) portal and is helping me move you to the next stage of your development. You are here to work with and be a part of a diverse group of people who will transform the status quo. We all need to be part of something—none of us can do it alone—so we are neurologically hardwired to connect with others. The industrious and persistent ants show that if you collaborate with others, you will achieve your goal. The Full Moon is here to activate your intuitive abilities and help you uncover any hidden agendas that might slow you down. Be passionate and take risks. This is not the time to play it safe. Whatever has gotten you to the place you are in now (positive or negative) has been exactly what was needed. The sunrise is giving you clarity, focus, and passion. This fresh new day shines a light on projects and ventures destined to produce abundance. The three (solid and stable) wise tortoises give you determination and endurance to finish anything you start at this time. There is a reason why you are drawn to these new endeavors in the first place. It is so vital that you be very specific with what you want because "what you put your attention to manifests" and "what you resist persists." Write down some affirmations—they are the first step to successful manifesting.

The more you do this, the more these frequencies are anchored in the current timeline. The waterfall beckons you to release anything that is not serving you—especially old negative habits. The most loving thing you can do is to learn to forgive yourself and others. Forgiveness clears up old karma and dissolves long-standing energy cords with others. Since the day you were born, you have been storing experiences and beliefs in your energy field, creating what I call cellular memories. The only way these unconscious habits can be treated is to send them unconditional love. Slow and steady, never give up and never waiver in your resolve to heal yourself and the world. Put your trust and faith in me, Amethyst, and I will rock your world!

Affirmations

I only do what feels right.

I am able to let go of all that is not serving me at this time.

*I am excited to embrace all the good luck and
success that is entering my life.*

AMMONITE
The Ancient Emancipator
Change, Evolution, and Personal Growth

I am Ammonite, a semiprecious stone created from living creatures, and I help to improve your breath. I am actually an ancient mollusk that lived millions of years ago and fossilized into beautiful shapes. My coiled external shell is similar to that of the modern nautilus. In this image, my two halves sit on the bottom shelves on either side of the fetus. You have chosen this card because you need to release the past. I can help you filter out unhealthy situations that come your way through my many chambers. And because of the highly oxygenated environment I lived in, I symbolize energy, strength, and longevity. My powerful name originates from the Egyptians, who thought my shape mirrored the ram's twisting horns worn by the god Ammon. When you hold me in your hands, you can feel a connection to ancient history (possibly a past life?). The cosmic energy I have absorbed for thousands of years stimulates, inspires, and motivates you. What is so striking about me are my beautiful spiral formations. Spirals symbolize evolution and progression. Like me, you must go through significant changes, but these changes will be gradual. And while this is happening, you will easily adapt to a new and exciting timeline (and version of yourself). I am not bragging, but I am known to attract good fortune and success when you wear me. In this image, I have been made into earrings. Earrings are associated with the feminine, financial stability, and your place in life. My earrings assure you that you will be noticed for the creative and hard work you have done for such a long time.

Joining our journey are the gray wolf, a purple rose, and a fetus. Because the wolf is a teacher and a trailblazer, he comes to you when you need guidance. This wolf says to trust your inner voice (also known as your intuition) when making decisions; this will help you develop the strength and self-confidence necessary to venture into new territory. Wolves are very social and loyal. They balance family time with alone time. Before leaving the pack, they ensure all responsibilities are handled and all are safe. Rituals are also very important to them, like howling at the Moon and greeting pack members upon return. And they regularly find time to jump and frolic with each other. An important message the wolf brings is to slow down and be mindful of your schedule and daily routines. What are your rituals and habits? Do you perform them automatically without thinking, or do you honor them? Are you having fun with family and friends? Are you enjoying yourself? Do you laugh?

The purple rose reminds you to see all the beauty in your life. Purple, in general, is the color of good judgment and purpose. Apart from being symbols of love at first sight, purple roses also represent enchantment. But the rose has a more mysterious history. It was an ancient form of the modern-day "Do Not Disturb" sign. A rose was placed on the door when secrecy was required. Only the rich (like royalty) had access to roses and used them as legal tender. What secrets are you keeping? The fetus reminds you how charmed your new life will be because it is being birthed from the rose (love) and the guidance and protection of me, Ammonite. With my divine magic, the past and present collide, squaring the circle and activating your sacred cosmic divinity.

Affirmations

I allow myself to be open to the process of change and embrace it fully.

I am always connected with my galactic family and feel safe and loved.

I am strong when I am alone, and I am even stronger when I am with my community.

AQUAMARINE
The Brilliant Partner
Clarity, Tranquility, and Youthful Vitality

I am Aquamarine, a greenish-blue form of beryl, and I feel your concerns. In my natural form, I am transparent and come in either blue, blue-green, or sea-green colors. I am a stone of the sea, renewal, and springtime. I bring clarity and balance to any issues you are facing. In this image, I hover above the two profiles to see the big picture. You have chosen this card because you need to speak your truth. I can help you do that by building your self-confidence. How? You need to learn to breathe *deeply*. Slowing down your breath will cleanse you of negative thoughts, allowing you to tap into the frequencies of peace and tranquility. Keep me close to activate deep compassion, trust, and even psychic abilities. All the answers you seek are floating just beneath the surface of your emotions. I am here to encourage you to dive in and enjoy the swim.

Joining our journey are two dolphins, two blue crabs, a white orchid, a white gardenia, Jupiter, the Earth, two Egyptian columns, and the hands of Source. The dolphins are all about cooperation, friendship, and fun. They want you to laugh, discover, and play (I don't mean with phones or computers!). We all knew how to play in the past, but very few of us partake in it now. Play is more about spending quality time with friends, family, pets, and even nature. George Bernard Shaw was spot-on when he wrote, "We don't stop playing because we grow old; we grow old because we stop playing." Adults who play reap tremendous benefits—spiritually, mentally, and physically. Remember, laughter is the best medicine. The ancient columns support and balance the Earth and Jupiter. Together, they send out healing vibrations that magnify strength, security, and good fortune. The crabs remind you to set appropriate boundaries, allowing you to stay afloat during this transitional time.

Let the striking white orchid teach you how to cultivate beauty, refinement, elegance, and good taste. Indulge in that which makes you feel special, and surround yourself with people who appreciate you for who you are. The more you feel good about yourself, the more you will exude divine charisma and become a beacon of inspiration for others. When the lovely gardenia is nearby, its sweet heavenly fragrance permeates your soul and inspires you. This inspiration could initiate a strong physical attraction with someone you always see—right in front of you. Maybe the relationship has not revealed itself to you yet, or, perhaps, you are keeping it secret—because the gardenia is all about secret love. Meditate with me, Aquamarine, and let me mirror what it's like to shine. Together, we will restore and rebuild a more healthy, kindhearted, and loving reality. Have courage. The hands of Source are always there to steady and guide you.

Affirmations

My destiny is to love and be loved.

I am a brilliant star, and my energy burns bright.

I am proud of who I am and acknowledge my inner and outer beauty

BRAZILIANITE
The Atlantean Amplifier
Creativity, Wisdom, and Intention Amplifier

I am Brazilianite, a rare yellow-green phosphate mineral that forms over feldspar, and I worship you. I come in chartreuse yellow, pale yellow, yellow-green, and colorless varieties. I am perched on top of a pyramid and connect you with ancient energies. You have chosen this card because you want to access divine wisdom, knowledge, and power. I can help. By stimulating your solar plexus, I move your thoughts into physical form (I learned this in Atlantis!). I radiate with intense energy—so fierce that it signals your brain neurons to turn on your innate powers and insights (intuition). I act as a conduit, stimulating and awakening information stored in your cellular structure—information like your Atlantean past life. Hold me in your hands. Stare deeply into my crystals. What do you sense and feel? Create an imaginary link with me and then think and speak any thoughts you want to manifest. This process works because I act as an intention amplifier. For example, if you desire a new relationship, look into my crystals while picturing the event taking place. It will help create a matching vibrational link. Remember, you cocreate with the matrix (God, the Universe, Physics, etc., however you see it), and you can ultimately change your life. All it takes is a disciplined mind.

Joining our journey are a margay cat, a barn owl, a pair of Gouldian finches, an African daisy, brain neurons, a Sun (Taygeta), pyramids, and three human figures. A sleepy, perhaps healing margay rests comfortably on a dendrite. It sees the world as a dream within the physical. Margays go by their intuition and feelings just as much as their sense of smell and taste. You need to do that too. Since margays have excellent night vision, they remind you that it is not as dark as you think—you can always see where you are going. The light in this image comes from the star Taygeta, located in the constellation of Taurus. This star is home to the Pleiadians—who were quite possibly the architects of the human brain. In the past, our ancestors interacted with these high masters who guided us to improve and accelerate our evolution. The figures holding on to the brain neurons are Pleiadians in the act of manipulating human brain cells. I believe they are here to assist humanity with the process of spiritual transformation.

The colorful finches have come to tell you that it is never too late to follow your passion and dreams. There is always time to live the life you deserve. The barn owl sees everything that is going on. Its heart-shaped face is not only distinctive and pretty. It actually directs sound to its ears, much like a satellite dish picks up signals to transmit to your television. This is why these owls are associated with strong clairvoyant abilities. Many pyramids line the horizon. Pyramids are associated with spiritual development—but they are much more. These unique structures are not tombs, like some archaeologists postulate, but more like amplifiers and transmitters. They have shown up in your life to help you see that you are not alone and have been heard. The beauty of the African daisy is that it is a wildflower; it doesn't need to be planted by anyone. Its message is to be independent and know you can succeed on your own. I, Brazilianite, want you to believe in yourself and your creative abilities. They are out of this world!

Affirmations

Yes, I can, I am sure of it!

I am ready, willing, and able to do what I need to do.

I can see clearly now; I can see all obstacles in my way.

CARNELIAN
The Assertive Motivator
Action, Luck, and Zest for Life

I am Carnelian, a member of the chalcedony family (a type of quartz), and I see your potential. I vary from semiopaque to translucent and can be various shades of red or amber. But most know me for my fiery red energy that, once picked up, is hard to put down. My intense pigment comes from the presence of iron oxide. In this image, two pieces of me sit on top of a dimensional box. You have chosen this card because you want more passion and pizazz in your life. I can help you with that because I symbolize action, audacity, and courage. I can reach you on a deep level and help you clear away layers of heavy energies that are not necessarily yours but have found their way into your aura (energy field). My buttery smooth surface and reddish color feel soothing and stimulating simultaneously. That is because I also symbolize warmth and love. When you need a little support, let me protect and guide you. I can breathe life back into any special projects you have put on the back burner. I will strengthen your resolve and self-confidence, allowing you to make it to the finish line. If you want to be noticed, wear me.

Joining our journey are two cardinals, a red rose, a tabby cat, the Crescent Moon, the Sun, the North Star, and a fairy named Kira. Fairies symbolize spirituality, feminine energy, and childhood.

Kira asks you to be forgiving, nurturing, compassionate, and loving. She has come into this dimension to let you know that you have a purpose here on Earth—as one of the many lightworkers. This is because the name *Kira* in Sanskrit and Hebrew means "beam of light." In Russian, it means "leader of the people." So it is clear to me that no matter what you do in this life, you are more influential than you realize. Your positive, loving energy radiates and touches others profoundly. The trees growing out of Kira's head represent stability and safety. "When the roots grow deep, there is no reason to fear the wind," says an African proverb. Kira is presenting you with a red rose. When someone like Kira offers you this beauty, take it. There's enchantment in the air. Don't be surprised if a new love shows up!

The two cardinals are messengers, connecting loved ones in the spirit world with you here on Earth. They carry your prayers and questions back to Source. Let these strong and vibrant birds increase your personal power. Cardinals help to strengthen your resolve and are good to call upon when you are feeling a bit down. Focusing on their energy gives you a shot of adrenaline and reminds you of your soul's purpose. Their bright red color is associated with determination, passion, and power. Red also physically increases your respiration and blood pressure—getting you ready to win! No wonder it's a favorite of people in charge. Sing your beautiful song to the world and know that you can call on the cardinal for passion, self-confidence, and renewal. Cats are masters at setting boundaries and being in the present moment. You need to follow their example. This cute tabby kitten is totally focused on you. It knows you have an unexplored aptitude or talent for something unique and extraordinary. The Crescent Moon and the Sun appear together because each balances the other— feminine and masculine. Sometimes you need to be strong and forceful and focus on the outer world; at other times, you need to be soft and gentle and go inward for answers. So let me, Carnelian, and the North Star balance your journey and be loving beacons of light guiding you to your true home in the stars.

Affirmations

*I set clear intentions and accomplish everything
I set out to do.*

*I am courageous, confident, and creative,
and I am determined to succeed!*

*I can easily find my way home—I tune in to
the vibrations of respect, appreciation, and love.*

CELESTITE
The Heavenly Meditator
Mindful, Psychic, and High Vibrations

I am Celestite, a type of strontium sulfate mineral (commonly used in fireworks!) that naturally occurs inside certain geodes, and I elevate your spirit. I am most often found in beautiful shades of pale celestial blue, but I can also be pink, pale green, pale brown, gray, or even colorless. In this image, my egg-like shape is placed between two blue herons and is being held up by angelic beings. I am associated with your crown chakra, helping you connect and communicate with the higher realms—the home of the angels. You have chosen this card because you want to have an explosive, mystical experience. I can help you because I am made up of the same element that is mixed with metal to create some of the spectacular blue fireworks you see. But at the same time, my sky-blue color helps the softer side of me come out. Hold me in your hands to feel an instant calm and clarity. This allows you to move through the world in a gentle, grounded manner. Journey with me while doing an open-eyed meditation and explore my fascinating crystal chambers. Move through these spiritual spaces and experience celestial energy you have never felt before. Don't be surprised if you find me, your guardian angel, at home there, dreaming of your company.

Joining our journey are two blue herons, a borage flower and two buds, some grass, the Sun, the Moon, and twenty-two angelic helpers. These twenty-two beings are helping you to find your way. By holding up the celestite, they are showing you how to feel calmer and more patient in challenging situations. They are also showing you that working with others is beneficial and productive. They recommend collaborating with others when dealing with daunting projects or situations. This is because twenty-two is a master number and very powerful. It is called the master architect. The clouds are parting, revealing an entire new way of being. Clouds are like the thoughts in your mind. They don't last long. They are of the moment, and then the moment passes and they are gone. Clouds remind us to stay in the present. The following quotation illustrates this concept beautifully: "You can't go back and change the beginning, but you can start where you are and change the ending" (C. S. Lewis).

The two blue herons are standing straight and strong. These stable birds have shown up to help you stay balanced and determined. When they appear, good fortune and happy times are imminent. This is because herons appear in the spring after the winter has receded. Symbolically, this means that you have endured cold, hard times, but the longer spring days will warm up your luck. The borage flower and buds are known for their courage and audacity. This unique, prickly flower has five blue petals and five green ones. They form a star! Like you! These ten petals reinforce the flower's symbolic meaning of being a leader. Ten also means the end of one cycle and the beginning of another. The two buds agree that new life is manifesting for you soon. Be bold, take your time, think things through, and then go for it! The Sun will energize your passion and the Moon will reveal some necessary information. The beach grass and the angels remind you that you are part of a larger network. I, Celestite, and the angels, connect you with the heavenly realm. There we help you "build" a new timeline for a new Earth. With faith, trust, and positive thinking, we can create a new matrix—a matrix of heavenly love.

Affirmations

I am always connected to my angelic twin.

My higher purpose is to be here on this planet and love all I meet.

I breathe in peace and release any stress I have stored in my body.

CHAROITE
The Spiritual Charmer
Authenticity, Balance, and Deep Transformation

I am Charoite, a potassium, barium, calcium strontium, hydrogen silicate mineral, and I dispel negativity. I am rare (only found in Siberia, Russia) and special, like you (there is only one you!). My purple color palette (from lilac to deep purple) makes you feel like royalty, reminding you that you are inherently powerful! In this image, my beads are hanging from a dimensional movie screen. You have chosen this card because you want to release old baggage. I can help with that. The swirling patterns that dance across my surface act as intense agitators (like a washing machine cycle). They churn and purify any deep unconscious beliefs floating around and bring them to the surface. This allows you to release annoying repetitive thoughts that keep you locked in fear. I also take on mischievous astral beings that hang around you and remove them from your etheric body. When you are ready for a shift (and to stand out for your creativity), keep me nearby!

Joining our journey are four dragonflies, a lotus flower, the Eye of God, a dimensional movie screen, two curtains, and the symbol for Jupiter. You are starting a new chapter in your life. Old ways of thinking and acting that are not serving you are falling away, and a new way of seeing is coming into alignment. Trust that there is a higher order bringing you exactly what you need to restore balance. I am here to give you a push in the direction you need to go, and the dragonflies will keep you in balance. They have the ability to see around things by looking from different angles. Using their ability to transform colors and light by reflecting and refracting them, dragonflies show you that life, like light, can bend, shift, and adapt in various ways. The dragonflies' magic allows you to see through life's illusions when you embrace your natural intuitive abilities.

The lotus flower has shown up to help you stay on the spiritual path. In general, the lotus is symbolic of rebirth, peace, and enlightenment, but in addition to its spiritual meaning, the lotus is also a symbol of good fortune and peace. It energizes and inspires people because its beauty originates from dark, murky, muddy waters— like hardships that have been overcome. Because this flower is being shown in a theater on a movie screen, it is reflecting the story of your spiritual life. It is asking you to step back and view who you are and what you are doing objectively. What is playing on your life screen at this stage of your development? Peek through your curtains and be open to seeing the true movie of your life. Are you an observer or an active participant? What role will you be playing? Are you being an artist by speaking in your own creative voice, or do you edit your performance for others? Whose values are you living by—your own or theirs? Whatever beliefs and patterns you currently have, be open to reviewing their effectiveness and how they serve you. It might be time to let them go and embrace something new. The two curtains indicate that it is time to break free from something in your life, such as people and/or habits, and exercise your creative side. The Eye of God (your Higher Self, or soul) will help you reflect and see a new vision for yourself. This spiritual portal transports you to an entirely new life and future. Jupiter and I say to have fun, let go, and share your life with the world (if not the universe!). You will succeed. You are perfect!

Affirmations

I rise through any predicament with grace and beauty.

I am willing to go deeper into my "story" to find the truth.

I am an independent person who is in the world but not of the world.

CHRYSANTHEMUM STONE
The Karmic Liberator
Intuition, Optimism, and Akashic Records

I am Chrysanthemum Stone, formed about 270 million years ago at the bottom of an ancient ocean, and I adore you. High temperatures and intense pressures of rich organic mud created my "flower." It consists of celestite, calcite, feldspar, and andalusite, while my black base is composed of dolomite, gypsum clay, limestone, and porphyry. In this image, I am centered in the Sun and radiate its strength and power. Many believe me to be a stone of passion, purpose, wealth, and honor. You have chosen this card because you are a beautiful soul experiencing challenging situations. You also want to feel joy again. I can help you reset your energy grid. Hold me in your hands when meditating and burrow deep into your intuition (matrix, Higher Self, or soul). Honor all thoughts (negative and positive) that come to the surface and release them. Together we will unearth layers of accumulated karma that help you break free from the past. You are here at this time to work out issues balancing the mind and heart. Previously, your mind or ego was in charge. But now, you must overcome the tendency to rationalize experience rather than just trust your heart. Let go of any concerns about others' opinions. No one knows what is good for you except you! Every conscious moment is a map of your state of mind—frozen in time forever. This map is called the Akashic Record. What do you want your Akash to look like? Why have you come here at this time? To learn to love, of course!

Joining our journey are two eagles, two groundhogs, a white chrysanthemum flower, a cherry tree, Jupiter, the Sun, the Crescent Moon, an ouroboros, and an ankh. The ouroboros and ankh remind you that you are immortal; your life is just one expression of Source (God). The cherry tree is about seeing the beauty in nature's cycles (such as reincarnation—beginnings and endings). But reincarnation is not what it seems to be. Yes, we do come back, but that is because we are caught in an energetic web at the behest of others. We need to wake up from our spiritual amnesia and realize we are only meant to be released into Source's power and nothing else. The groundhogs want you to dig deep into your inner world and bring light to things that are currently in the dark. They believe you have untapped hidden abilities. The mother groundhog has great aspirations for her baby and you. She wants you to revise your life story, but remember to include your dreams this time. No matter what your age or where you are in your life, now is the time to connect with your true life's purpose. How do you know when you have found it? It's simple. You will be filled with joy and unconditional love, and your heart will soar. Jupiter will also reward you with good luck, abundance, and success. Feel the intuitive frequencies of the feminine Crescent Moon gently illuminate the direction you need to go. But you will need the eagle's sharp vision and unwavering intent to empower you. Buddha said it best, "If we could see the miracle of a single flower clearly, our whole life would change." So help me, Chrysanthemum Stone, water your miraculous life with unconditional and eternal love—and see it blossom.

Affirmations

*Whatever I can imagine with my heart and mind,
I can create.*

*I easily navigate the material and spiritual worlds
and feel comfortable in both.*

*I allow creative energy to burst out of me and reach
every part of this dimension.*

CHRYSOCOLLA MALACHITE
The Confidence Builder
Calming, Order, and Mother Nature

I am Chrysocolla Malachite, a poetic blend of chrysocolla (a copper silicate) and malachite (a copper carbonate), and I am the guardian of your heart. I am also part of a stone known as Eilat stone (named after the city where it was once mined). My superpowers come from the hypnotic mixture of gorgeous deep turquoise-colored circles (sometimes mixed with brown) floating in a background of deep green. These energetic swirls help calm your anxieties and lessen your fears. In this image, I am being held up by the life force of guardians connected with the Sun and the Moon. You have chosen this card because you are weary. You want to quicken your spiritual evolution on this planet. I can help you. I strongly connect with Mother Nature because I am birthed from her soul. Hold me when you meditate to experience a closer relationship with her. I help make blissful order out of chaos by removing disempowering thoughts from your energetic field—but you must work with me. It is time to develop confidence in your decision-making abilities by trusting your gut feelings (otherwise called your intuition). Doing this will allow your psychic abilities and dreams to awaken.

Joining our journey are the Sun, the Full Moon, a white wolf, two voles, two dragonflies, a fly, and a red rose. The Sun (clarity) and the Full Moon (mystery), beckon you to leave the past behind and traverse any walls you have put up. These could be from past upsets you have kept inside and, brick by brick, built a solid barrier to hide them. Take the walls down and be free. The white wolf helps you be brave and stay on course during the process. Although the wolf mates for life and is extremely loyal, it is on a solitary path to discover its soul plan. It must learn to balance its desire to be free with its responsibility to others. Like the wolf, you must dance to your own tune while functioning on your journey here (limiting exposure to negative beliefs and judgments as best you can).

Dragonflies want you to transform your life story by stepping out of your comfort zone. This allows you to see a new ending. The fly and voles teach you that although they look small and vulnerable, they know they are intelligent and invincible. So are you! Their motto is illustrated by Martin Luther King's words: "If I cannot do great things, I can do small things in a great way." The voles also teach you to be sensitive and alert to your surroundings. Listen to what is happening around you because the mysterious Moon could be hiding something. They are nudging you out of your complacency and want you to tap into your creativity. Like the voles, keep busy doing what you love. The fly says to speed things up. It wants you to be gutsy and look for innovation in unusual places. The Sun is always willing to create and take a chance, but it says to be successful, you must be persistent. Always remember that you shine as brightly as the greatest stars in the galaxy. The loving red rose says every choice you make matters—make sure it comes from the heart. Let me, Chrysocolla Malachite, give you the self-confidence you need to accomplish what you came here to do. Wherever you are, remember you are sharing the same home planet and the same oxygen with every great person who has lived, is living, and will live. It's not fate that brought you to this point; it's destiny.

Affirmations

I believe I have what it takes!

Fear is only an illusion; the only power it has is what I give it.

My heart is open, and any walls I have constructed in the past come tumbling down.

DANBURITE
The Sweet Enlightener
Celestial, Karma, and Sweet Disposition

I am Danburite, a form of calcium boron silicate, and I am your guardian angel. I am usually colorless, like quartz, but can also be either pale yellow or yellowish brown. My distinct features (such as my cleavage and fluorescence), help to tell us apart. I can be a bit pricey and tricky to find, but I am well worth the search. I am a messenger from the angelic realm and I come from the divine heart. In this image, there are three crystals on the ground; the two clear ones are being held by the dormice and the brownish one is connected with the angelic being in the center. You have chosen this card because you want to calm the constant mind chatter that makes you feel unbalanced. I can help you. My sweet disposition links your heart and crown chakras and activates other chakras you didn't even know you had! Let me heal you of old deep wounds and clear out past karma. Keep me near when you meditate or sleep, and I will generate a calming vibrational force field surrounding your space. This force field is possible because I plug you into a higher consciousness that aligns with your individual energetic blueprint. In other words, I activate the process or path of your enlightenment.

Joining our journey are two dormice, a tern, a warbler, a hedgehog, a maple leaf, bird-of-paradise flowers, mandevilla vines wrapped around a fence, Venus, the Sun, and a winged angelic being. This unique being emerges out of my central crystal and carries my frequency. The beautiful white arctic tern flaps its wings in excitement and recognition of her arrival. Like me, this pure white bird is a messenger linking you with the heavenly realm. White is considered the color of ancestors, clarity, innocence, and new beginnings. Trust that this bird from the angelic realm is whispering positive and uplifting messages in your inner ears. These messages will lead you to your purpose here on Earth. A new chapter in your life is about to unfold. Expect the unexpected and allow the miraculous to happen. Pablo Picasso said it well, "The meaning of life is to find your gift. The purpose of life is to give it away."

Have faith that all is possible, but realize that you have to allow it to happen. Everything is as it is supposed to be; you are in the right place at the right time. The dormice encourage you to rely on your intuition more than you currently do—and adapt to all that is going on. One way is to stay grounded in the Earth (Gaia). Gaia's energy is healing, balancing, and stabilizing. The hedgehog (like the fence) reminds you to set your boundaries and be very discerning about who and what you let in. It protects you like a mother, bringing you inner peace and pure happiness. The warbler helps clear your throat and find the song you came here to sing. The mandevilla vines give you the strength and direction to find your true friends and community. The bird-of-paradise flower helps you find heaven on Earth— and the Sun, Venus, and maple leaf want you to know how strong you are. They want you to believe in love . . . again. Be grateful for everything in your life. Remember, you are always protected with a force field of love. Your angelic spirit guide and I, Danburite, are always watching over you. Feel the guidance and support we are sending. Believe in divine magic and trust that we are but a thought away.

Affirmations

I always have and always will be connected with my ancestors.

I can do anything I want to do when I align with the energy of the Divine.

I am here to help change planet Earth to the heavenly home I know she can be.

EPIDOTE
The Dream Walker
Enhance, Increase, and Magnifying Thoughts

I am Epidote, an aluminum iron silicate mineral that occurs in marble and schistose rocks, and I magnetize your thoughts. This is because I can contain small amounts of ferrous oxide. I am a pearly transparent to nearly opaque gemstone and come in shades of green, yellow, gray, grayish white, greenish black, and black. In this image, there are small pistachio-like tumbled pieces of me floating in the nighttime sky. My name comes from the Greek word *epidosis,* meaning "to add to or increase." This explains why you need to be careful around me because I amplify any thoughts and emotions you are experiencing (remember the law of attraction— what you give out you get back). If you focus on high-frequency words such as *love* and *compassion,* that is what I will intensify. If you focus on low-frequency words such as *hate* and *anger,* you will find these emotions escalating as well. But don't worry. In general, I will help raise your frequency and reduce any negativity you are holding in your body (making it easier to feel positive). I do this by gently helping you release any patterns that have formed due to past hurts or wounds. I am also known as a very powerful dream stone. Sleep with me under your pillow and I will enhance your dream cycles as well as lucid dreaming. Let me remind you to always do your best and you will be prosperous.

Joining our journey are a red, green, and gold labyrinth; a green Full Moon; a piglet; five gold coins; and the twelve zodiac constellations. Labyrinths are ancient symbols that represent a spirit's journey on this Earth (literally). They take you on a meandering path of faith, determination, patience, intention, and bravery. The striking labyrinth has manifested here to slow you down and encourage mindfulness. Its strong red color gives you passion to continue on the journey no matter how frustrating, while its deep green color allows you to remain calm while running into walls. The golden boundaries dazzle and tempt you every step of the way. No matter what you are experiencing, there is an end to this puzzle. You will solve it. But don't take anything for granted—everything is here to teach you something. Helping you on your quest is a beautiful green Full Moon illuminating your way. This Moon symbolizes growth, renewal, and rebirth. It wants you to know that some form of abundance, fertility, and/or security will soon be revealed. Be patient. Any challenging events currently taking place in your life will soon make sense and might even be more positive than you think.

The happy pig represents financial stability and prosperity (ever heard of a piggy bank?). The gold coins obviously represent good fortune as well. But, because there are five of them, they are also associated with spiritual evolution, self-consciousness, and personal freedom. Their message is that wealth comes from your state of mind—your belief system. The more you appreciate everything you have, the more you will have to appreciate. The stars have aligned for you, and no matter what sign you were born under or where you are on your path, you are being divinely guided. You are a brave soul at the threshold of a new beginning. You have done an amazing job at home, work, and/or school. You have satisfied some rules, reached for something special, and/or achieved your goals. Your accomplishments will be acknowledged, and you will get recognition for all your hard work. This world is a better place because of you, and you have helped more than you will ever know. Let me, Epidote, congratulate you on a job well done. The universe is applauding you.

Affirmations

I move passionately in the direction of my dreams.

My abundant creativity flows through me like a stream of consciousness.

I am surrounded by good fortune—I just need to open my eyes to see it.

FLUORITE
The Psychic Releaser
Comforting, Intuitive, and Otherworldly Talents

I am Fluorite, a form of calcium fluoride (part of the family of halide minerals), and I connect with your mind. In my pure state I am colorless and transparent, but impurities (usually hydrocarbons) can make me very colorful. I am available in shades of black, brown, purple, blue, yellow, green, and even occasionally in pink. When you hold my smooth surfaces, I soothe and comfort you. In this image, I am being handed to you by the hand of Source from another dimensional realm. You have chosen this card because you want and need a champion during these challenging times. You have found one. I help you connect to your inner and outer self-confidence by awakening your intuitive and psychic abilities. Close your eyes and visualize walking up and receiving your gift. I will release and transmute any confusing thoughts, conflicting ideas, and/or negative emotions that get in your way. I also act like a vacuum cleaner, suctioning anything that is not for your highest and best good. Carry me in your pocket and feel waves of calming energy move through your body. Meditate with me and strengthen your connection with the spiritual realm.

Joining our journey are a hummingbird, a frog, a mink, some ladybugs, two ring of fire sunflowers, a yin-yang symbol, a monarch butterfly, the Full Moon, and the molecular formula for oxytocin. Your message is about accepting change and learning to tap into and connect with universal bonding and love (the formula hovers above you). But love is more than just a song lyric; it is the structure of the universe. You are the architect of your life. Rumi says, "Your task is not to seek for love, but merely to seek and find all the barriers within yourself that you have built against it." It is time to wake up to your truth. There is a new normal—one where you are eternally balanced, flexible, and adaptable (yin-yang). Here, you will continuously learn from your lessons and create a different world— a different timeline. The mink says to tap into your private side and always think for yourself. Don't let others make up your thoughts; they are falsehoods. Your monarch butterfly will help you transform your current life into something beautifully unrecognizable. Just like the caterpillar who releases its old body and welcomes a totally new one, you too must have faith in the process.

The seeds of creativity within the sunflower will light you on fire. With the frog bringing you new opportunities, your life will be renewed and become more meaningful in ways you would never have imagined. The Full Moon has secrets—but not for long. As you ascend, your unconscious programming will be revealed. Any looping (repeating cycles) will cease, and you will see clearly for the first time. The hummingbird wants you to live your life with joy and laughter. It says to adapt and adjust so you can help bring happiness to your current timeline. The act of revolution is afoot, but not in the way you think. It takes place in the mind, not in the 3D world. Power is in the way you think. Max Planck, the quantum physicist, said, "When you change the way you look at things, the things you look at change." Change your way of thinking, and you become a powerful wizard. Walk the magical red carpet with me, Fluorite, and touch the chemical compound of passion and love . . . it will turn you on!

Affirmations

I am here to spread love and light to all I meet.

I release any hidden programming and welcome clarity.

Without labels, life expands to an infinite number of possibilities.

GARNET
The Sensual Believer
Commitment, Relationships, and Believing in Yourself

I am Garnet, a silica mineral, and I am committed to our relationship. I am part of a large mineral family named after all my colors. These minerals are found throughout the planet in metamorphic, igneous, and sedimentary rocks. I have a smooth glassy surface, and my sensual deep red color comes from iron. In this image, a sugar glider is pushing me out of a solar portal. You have chosen this card because you need to believe in yourself. I am here for you. I will help you focus on self-confidence and meaningful relationships. If you want more love (and sexuality) in your life, wear me near your heart chakra. I help you form new relationships and strengthen old ones. And since I am formed under pressure, I help you handle stressful relationships at work. When you hold me close, feel how calm your breathing gets. That is because my inner structure is symmetrically balanced, making it easier to resist negative forces. I also bring order, passion, creativity, and strength into your life. If you need a powerful stone to help ward off things that go bump in the night—I am the one for you!

Joining our journey are a sugar glider, a white phalaenopsis orchid, seven ladybugs, a small pika, a green crab spider, a web, the Full Moon, and some space molecules. The sugar glider and I want you to "go where no man has gone before." Sounds like *Star*

Trek? You're right. You are here to take risks with people, places, and things—and connect with the stars (both literally and figuratively). Navigate your life without any fear. Steady yourself, take a huge leap, and fly through space. The impressive white orchid is about reproduction and pollination. Its underground tubers and exotic flowers symbolically align with sexuality, virility, fertility, and self-pollination. This translates into knowing how to love yourself so much that you can birth your own "offspring" through creative projects, jobs, and dreams. I am assisting the white orchid in helping you let go of outdated beliefs accumulated since birth. The result is a new, improved version of yourself. The emotional pika is industrious, proactive, and innovative. It connects with fifth-dimensional knowledge and helps release unproductive third-dimensional ways of thinking. It encourages you to act on positive ideas and strategies that will help shift our planet.

The huge orange Sun appears behind me and emanates creative, happy, successful, and healing frequencies. You tune in to these wavelengths and gain limitless energy. Delve into your inner fusion reactor and release that which is too heavy! The Moon is cryptic and secretive—but something is being revealed. Some past cycle in your life has finished, and an unspecified direction is starting. This change could involve something in your life that was interrupted. The tiny green spider serves as a reminder that your choices construct your life and weave a web that either serves you or enslaves you (karma). Like me, the seven tiny, red ladybugs bring you security, self-confidence, and self-love. They believe if you think positive thoughts, you will attract good luck! Listen to the gentle call of the space molecules activating your passions. Their message triggers beneficial, dramatic changes and new opportunities. Are you ready? Yes! Live in the moment and glide over the poetry of time like you are skating on ice. First, learn to keep your balance; next find your creative groove; and then let go and soar. I, Garnet, will always be there to catch you.

Affirmations

I leap into the arms of fate, knowing she will catch me.

I tap into my higher mind and dissolve any limiting beliefs.

My passion fuels the universe and opens amazing portals.

HANKSITE
The Earthy Supporter
Cleansing, Grounding, and Heightened Sense of Reality

I am Hanksite, a rare potassium sulfate mineral, and I connect you with the Earth. I am commonly found beneath the surface, embedded in mud or drill cores. Due to my high sodium content, I taste quite salty. I may not be a very fancy crystal, but I am an important one. In this image, I am hovering above the blue planet (Earth) being supported by loving earthbound souls. You have chosen this card because you need to be grounded. I am a dense, heavy stone that helps you feel at home on this planet. Although I'm floating above the Earth, if you look closely, you can see all the loving earthbound souls supporting me. I am good at aiding in the realignment of your etheric chakra system. I merge with your aura, removing any harmful vibrations that attach to you as you go out and about. You will find that positive energy flows more naturally as you become more confident and optimistic. If you are shy, I help you feel more important since I remove old, outdated beliefs that keep you from progressing. In some ways, I rewire your thoughts so that you project only that which you want. Hold me over any area of your body that feels unbalanced and needs healing. Visualize it merging with your body, extinguishing any negativity. If you do this daily, you will find you are able to love, laugh, and prosper.

Joining our journey are a capybara, a beaver, two tulips, two honeybees, the Full Moon, a viaduct, the Earth with some inhabitants, and a shooting star. The capybara is like a colossal guinea pig weighing about 174 pounds! It seems intimidating, but it is quite gentle. It is also very social and loves to be petted. It does best when in a group and around lots of water (emotions). You may think you can do it alone, but capybara says you will function more efficiently with others nearby. This sensitive vegetarian wants you to get in touch with your feelings—observe and honor them, but don't let them control you. Capybaras work together to ensure the group's survival, especially the mothers who nurse any young who need it. It is essential for you and the planet that we all care for and help each other. The beaver says to follow your intuition when working on new projects. You have all the necessary talents needed to accomplish your goals. You don't need an engineering degree to build something—nor do you need to be a professional writer to write. Old academic standards are outdated, and you have access to new information at your fingertips—at any time. Tulips are one of the first flowers to grow in spring, making them a symbol of rebirth. And since there are two of them, the symbolism is all about balance, partnerships, and diplomacy. Perhaps you will renew or start a special relationship this spring? Remember, love is not outside of you—it emanates from you. You have to be loving to see love.

The honeybees want you to examine your productivity. Are you doing all you can to make your life more fertile? Bees are the symbol of accomplishing the impossible because aerodynamically, their bodies are too large for their wings and they should not be able to fly. They show that you, too, can achieve what seems impossible by being dedicated, working hard, and collaborating with others. The Moon is vibrating with mysterious energy and transmitting new information that will lead you to brilliant epiphanies. The viaduct symbolizes transition and change because it allows you to reach places you wouldn't normally be able to get to. Like the bees, it makes the impossible possible. Trust me, Hanksite, and I will help you build your dreams. You are up to the challenge. With the support of your home planet, and a shooting star overhead, your wishes will inevitably come true.

Affirmations

It is possible, it's just the way I look at it.

When I count the stars, I start with myself.

I am on the right track to my spiritual destination.

IOLITE
The Shamanic Navigator
Channel, Visionary, and Clear Vision

I am Iolite, a magnesium aluminum silicate, and I can guide you home. I am a variety of the transparent to translucent form of the mineral cordierite. My name, *ios,* comes from the Greek word meaning "violet." Because of my trichroism (luminous shifting shades of blue-violet color), I am called the Water Sapphire. In this image, I am in the center of the compass. You have chosen this card because you feel lost. I can help steer you in the right direction. This is because the Vikings, when sailing, used me as a light polarizer. I made it possible for them to determine the position of the Sun even on cloudy days. I will clear your vision too—by unblocking your third eye. This will enable you to better see and process your past, helping you to understand your present. You will find that this helps you accept and love who you are and what you are here to do. Hold me close to your pineal gland (between your eyes) when you need to enhance your intuition—or what I call pure thoughts. How beautiful it is to see and accept this inner genius.

Joining our journey are a compass with the four cardinal points, the Norwegian coastline, four ladybugs, an iris with its pupil, and intertwined branches. Built into your consciousness is a perfect intuitive compass. This compass always points to home. Symbolically, this means you can never get lost—you can always find your way back. Wherever you go, be patient; you have much to experience on your quest for understanding. Traditionally, the cardinal points symbolize wisdom for the north, spirit for the east, conclusions for the west, and beginnings for the south. But on this compass, south also relates to the word *love* (self-love, romantic love, familial love, and unconditional love). If you navigate the Norwegian coastline that surrounds the compass and head south, you will always experience smooth waters. And the four ladybugs sitting on the compass indicate that you will attract good luck in whichever direction you move. This is because these tiny beetles represent good fortune. Ladybugs are the vacuum cleaners of negative energy and will help you leave limiting energies behind. Since number four deals with stability, self-expression, and self-fulfillment, it teaches you that you are more creative and accomplished than you know.

The eye (iris and pupil) are similar to parts of a camera; they regulate how much light is let in. Metaphorically speaking, this relates to how much light or dark (positive or negative) energy you allow into your consciousness. You can control this energy with mindfulness. The undulating branches moving around the face of the compass weave in and out of life's challenges and still grow strong. They remind you to be flexible and persistent. Whatever direction you choose to go, embrace it—and may the wind be at your back. Team up with me, Iolite, and sail "your ship" past the known, into the unknown. As Andre Gide put it, "One doesn't discover new lands without consenting to lose sight, for a very long time, of the shore." The Vikings did it . . . and you can too!

Affirmations

*I may look fragile, but I am tougher
than I seem.*

*Any direction I travel, good luck, harmony,
and protection follow.*

*I may be a small dot on the universal map, but I am as
important as the largest celestial body.*

JASPER
The Optimistic Influencer
Inspirational, Resourceful, and Anything Is Possible

I am Polychrome Jasper, a sedimentary stone known as *chert,* and I encourage you to be resourceful. I am also called Desert Jasper because of my subtle earth tones (usually made up of red hematite inclusions and yellow, brown, green, and occasionally blue colors). I look like I was dropped into liquid, swirled around, and frozen in motion. Every piece of me is a creative abstract painting. In this image, the lion cub is resting on me. You have chosen this card because you need a muse—a source of inspiration. I can be that. Hold me in your hands when you meditate and feel me stimulate your creativity and imagination. It is important that you be true to yourself and your unique visions. Keeping a small piece of me with you helps you see the brighter side of things. This is because I connect you with the planet's heart and soul. I also clear blocked energy channels, allowing you to embrace life with the brakes off. My motto is that anything is possible.

Joining our journey are two lions, three foxes, four swallows, a magic lantern, a crystal ball, two balloons, the Moon (hidden by the clouds), and the Sun. Everything is shifting, and you are helping to create a blueprint for a new social system—one in which everyone counts and no one is more important than another. The lions tell you to summon the power of the Sun! His cub (like you) carries the wisdom of his lineage. Lions are kings and leaders. They are telling you that you have the ability to lead others and be a dominant force here on Earth. Your vibrant, positive energy is attractive to others. You have the ability to lift others up and help them to help themselves. The four swallows are on a vital mission. Long ago, ancient people believed that swallows ushered in springtime and new life (rebirth and new beginnings). Since four swallows represent creation, order, and determination, they want you to focus on something new. Also, their keen eyesight and exceptional flying abilities allow them to reach toward the Sun (life) and activate your passions. The young fox is brave and venturing out on its own. He is networking with a swallow (loyalty). Foxes are discriminating and skilled at staying invisible and below the radar when they want to be. This message is about taking risks with your creations but not sharing them until they are fully grown—and only with those you trust.

A magic lamp is set on the ledge between the two lions. What is a lamp but a device that gives off light (divine wisdom)? This lamp helps you navigate your way through illusion safely. Rub your unique lamp and summon an all-powerful wish-granting genie. You have the power to command anything you want from this servant. But be very, very careful when choosing your three wishes—you might just get what you ask for. Look into the crystal ball just beyond the lamp. Ask a question. What do you see? Trust your intuition and what comes into your mind's eye. You are bound to the Earth and gravity, but balloons are not. Balloons, therefore, represent the need to let go—to be free from restrictions. So release your loving, creative balloons and let your ideas soar to the sky. You are here to follow your passion and contribute your divine talents. Remember, your magic lamp gives you three wishes, and the Full Moon (just coming out from behind the clouds) gives you another. As Richard Bach said, "You are never given a wish without also being given the power to make it come true." Make your wishes and know that they will appear. I, Polychrome Jasper, will make sure they are colorful!

Affirmations

I wish for health, happiness, and love for all.

I respect all opinions and ideas; they are all valuable.

Compassion is the new treasure; love is the new gold.

KUNZITE
The Loving Savior
Harmonizing, Trust, and Unconditional Love

I am Kunzite, a lithium, aluminum, and silicate mineral part of the spodumene and pyroxene mineral families, and I feel your mental pain. My delicate colors (I come in light to medium pink and purple) are from trace amounts of manganese. I am a stone of unconditional and universal love. In this image, I appear in the nighttime sky. You have chosen this card to help you lift any negativity that has landed in your heart. I can easily do this. By merging with your soul, I connect you with ancient memories you have brought back to this incarnation. I help quiet these thoughts (allowing you to process them) by connecting you with the loving frequencies of the universal heart/mind. Place me over your heart chakra, and I will open its locked chambers with the power of trust and joy. You believe in me because you can feel my shield of protective energy surround you and neutralize anything that is not for your highest and best good. With the help of Source's love (and lithium), I can help mitigate addictions, imbalances, panic attacks, and/or chronic anxiety you may be experiencing. And when you need help with problematic relationships, picture my gentle energy merging with your auric field, uplifting and supporting you. This enables you to balance your emotions, allowing you to experience and reciprocate love.

Joining our journey are a pink grasshopper, a snake plant, ten yellow primrose wildflowers, four dandelions, a ladybug, and the Sun. Now is the time to jump for joy and catch your dreams. The ancient and wise grasshopper is related to the cricket. Remember Jiminy Cricket—who helped Pinnochio become a real boy by listening to his conscience? You, too, need to listen to the gentle, cheerful voice guiding you. If the grasshopper has hopped into your life, you need to trust in your intuition, not what comes to you from the outer world. Also, it wants you to "jump" forward and never look back! Many new things are waiting for you to create, discover, invent, and share with the world. Believe in luck. It's easier to manifest than you think.

The tiny red ladybug stands out wherever it lands. This is because its red color is so powerful. This beauty says that what you do will be noticed too. The snake plant will keep you healthy by adding more oxygen to your environment. This allows you to function your best. When this super plant shows up, it reminds you to take deep breaths and increase your oxygen intake. Your mind will be "sharper." Also, its long sharp blades earned it the nickname "mother-in-law's tongue." For you, this means being sensitive when speaking with others at home and work—you may not realize how you sound. Ten wildflowers are growing in the lush green grass all by themselves. They need little outside help. Their message is to believe in yourself and be more independent. Ten is the number of leadership and new beginnings. Maybe it is time to have your own space to grow and work—you don't need much. Walk in nature, feel the wind, and follow your heart. Blow on the dandelions to make all your wishes come true. The Sun rises on a new day of happiness, contentment, and self-confidence. What a great day this is going to be! Take a stroll with me, Kunzite, and fly away.

Affirmations

I can do it on my own—for now.

I breathe in the strength of the universe and exhale love.

My creative ideas are scattered by the wind and land in my heart.

LABRADORITE
The Grounded Invigorator
Revitalizing, Magic, and Spiritual Consciousness

I am Labradorite, a calcium-enriched feldspar, and I acknowledge how enchanted you are. I know this because I am special; I am a stone of magic. My beautiful iridescence is known as labradorescence. Labradorescence is a vibrant, natural optical effect that seems to light me up from the inside. This energy allows me to protect your aura and invigorate your entire body. Although I mainly come in brilliant blue and blue green, I sometimes appear with flashes of yellow and red. In this image, I am located in the neck of a torso, just below the white flower and balanced between the wings of an osprey. You have chosen this card because you need to see the truth about what you came here to do. I can speak about this because I am connected with the throat chakra—that is where I am most at home—like in this image. At the same time that I raise your spiritual consciousness, I also ground you to your soul purpose. If you find yourself a slave to work or anything else, I will ease the connection and help you find balance again. I help you believe in yourself—and the dreams encoded into you at birth. The longer you work with me, the more you'll feel your third eye open and your psychic abilities awaken. I don't want to boast, but I can boost your ability to sense the unknown through telepathy and clairvoyance. That is why I am the crystal of shamans, healers, and anyone wanting to help heal others.

Joining our journey are an osprey, a red panda, an almond tree in the shape of a human torso with one flower, ten almonds, eight pyramids, a Greek coin, Roman arches, and a Full Moon. The osprey has appeared to you today to let you know that you share its wings. Yes, you have wings—energetic ones. And you can fly! What does having wings mean? It means you are part of the family of light beings (the angelic realm). These wings help lift you from the ground and connect with your light body. Simply put, your light body is a vehicle that helps you graduate from your earthly human experience and return to Source. The osprey is carrying an ancient coin. Since a coin is round, it has a similar meaning to the circle— wholeness—connected to all that was and all that will be. Money is a form of energy—currency. And for money to grow, it must keep moving. And so must you. The red panda rests for a while on top of a white flower (new beginnings). It wants you to have patience while you find your way. It insists that you tap into your uniqueness and let it sparkle. It reminds you that when you are stressed, seek tranquility and peace of mind in nature and her spirits.

The Roman arches symbolize that you are crossing a new threshold. Reality is shifting for you, and what you once thought was true is now obsolete. Like the osprey whose self-confidence soars, you will one day see how important your talents are for the health of this planet. With this understanding, you will automatically heal yourself and others, love yourself and everyone you meet, respect all life-forms, and be joyfully happy. This card connects you to many past lifetimes. Chances are you lived in Egypt, Greece, or Italy. When you meditate, see if you remember. The Full Moon reminds you of the buried wisdom you still retain from all those lifetimes. Let me, Labradorite, help you take off into the past, present, and future. Together we will defy gravity and the laws of physics, and you will become the free spirit I know you are.

Affirmations

*I attract wealth and allow it to flow smoothly
and continuously.*

*I am part of a lineage that gives me strength,
identity, and creativity.*

*I plant my feet on the ground and sprout new ideas,
compassion, and love.*

LAPIS LAZULI
The Wisdom Keeper
Art, Honesty, and Enhancing Intellectual Ability

I am Lapis Lazuli, a metamorphic stone made up of lazurite, calcite, sodalite, and pyrite, and I encourage self-knowledge. My deep, celestial blue color, dotted with golden (pyrite) stars, has made me a beloved stone of ancient civilizations and royalty who believed I was connected with the gods. This is because I channel universal wisdom, spirit, and loyalty. In this image, I am being held by cosmic forces. You have chosen this card because you want to open your mind and experience enlightenment. I can help by enhancing and activating your third eye and psychic abilities. My reassuring celestial blue color links with your throat chakra, allowing you to better articulate what you experience. Hold or wear me and feel my soothing energies protect you from random and/or targeted psychic attacks. I also work on strengthening your immune system, lowering your blood pressure, and helping you sleep. My beauty and rare color motivated artists in the past to grind me into fine pigment and use me in their paintings. If you let me, I will synchronize your mind, body, and soul—and you will feel heavenly!

Joining our journey are the Eye of Horus, a scarab, two pyramids, two lotus plants with six flowers, virtual reality portals, the Sun, the stars, and a Christlike figure. The Eye of Horus represents protection, royal power, and good health. It symbolizes a well-known myth about Isis, Osiris, and Horus and is about the journey of enlightenment. But what is really fascinating about the shape of this amulet is that it is literally taken from the human brain. This all-seeing eye, or the third eye (as it is called), represents the pineal gland located in the center of the brain and decodes the central nervous system. Its important message to you is that the way to awaken mystical knowledge is to use your inner senses and not the egoic mind. The ancient Egyptians knew that nothing in the outer world could lead them to the truth. Another symbol of protection was the scarab. This purple beetle was linked to the cyclic nature of life and death (reincarnation) and compared to the rising and setting Sun. The Eye of Horus appears at present to show that you are at a crossroads—you have the choice of continuing on the same path as you have done for lifetimes or taking a new one aligned with your soul purpose and cosmic forces. The pyramids remind you that you are balanced; you have a solid base that can easily withstand all the many changes you are experiencing. They want you to know that you are supported by heaven and Earth. Six beautiful lotus flowers grow out of the murky, muddy waters and teach that you too can overcome adversity. No matter what your beginning, your ending will be triumphant—especially your finances! The powerful, creative Sun will help you burn through any distortion fields. It wants you to be a sovereign, free, and independent life force.

Virtual reality portals that manifested on either side of the figure have appeared here to propose that reality might not be what you think it is. The big question is, are we living in a virtual reality game? The answer is unknowable because, after watching videos of physicists working their magic with mathematical formulas, they couldn't prove that we don't live in one. Regardless, live your life with love and passion and it won't matter! Follow me, Lapis Lazuli, and the divine stars to enlightenment and know that you are the creator of your destiny.

Affirmations

*Yes, I know the truth, and the truth will
set me free.*

*It is time to acknowledge my nobility and see my
place in the universe.*

*I am here on a mission of unconditional love sent by
myself on the other side of the veil.*

MOLDAVITE
The Interplanetary Visitor
Acceleration, Synchronicity, and Shifting Your Life

I am Moldavite, a tektite, and I bring the light of knowledge into your life. I am a true child of the universe, for I am born in the stars and my outer form is shaped by my journey to Earth. As I fall from the heavens, the heat and flames melt my surface, creating undulating bifurcations and furrows. When I make an impact with Earth, the power creates green shiny, sculpted, wrinkled, lacelike surfaces (hence my name *Moldavite,* meaning "molten"). In this image, I am on the lower left, sitting on the ground just in front of the flames. You have chosen this card because you want to make a major shift in your life. I can help. Because of my high vibrational energy, many consider me a talisman here to serve humankind and aid in Earth's healing. If you are ready to accelerate your personal and spiritual evolution and feel a close connection with Universal Source, keep me close by. You might just experience fireworks! When you place me on your heart, I surround you with a vibrational field triggering daily synchronicities. I also activate dormant memories of why you chose to be here and neutralize the hypnotic commands from well-meaning people and the media that would keep you asleep.

Joining our journey are a chinchilla, two phoenix birds, a black woman, two spirit guides, some green grapes, an apple, a pink rose, two Greek columns, the Crescent Moon, and the Earth. The chinchilla has shown up to help you balance something in your life. It could possibly be about health and nutrition. This is because chinchillas have a sensitive digestive system and have to be careful what they eat. They recommend only nutritious food—cut back on any sugar, and just be smart before you put anything into your mouth. The Greek columns are sturdy and stable, and they are here to let you know your ideas are supported by some very strong and loving forces. But change is afoot. Many of the symbols in this painting are about releasing something. Between the phoenix birds, the fire, and me—you are being guided to let go of everything you once knew as "comfortable" and accept an entirely new life. Out of the fire emerge two spirit guides, letting you know you don't have to go through this stage alone—and there is even abundance (the apple and grapes) waiting for you. The heart-shaped rose says that you are going through an alchemical transmutation of matter into love. The huge Moon balanced on top of the rose and black woman symbolizes duality, femininity, and creativity. Its shape resembles a cradle. What new ideas, projects, proposals, wishes, and dreams do you want to birth and fill the cradle with? Maybe some innovative heart-based programs at work—ones that allow you to use your full range of talents? Open your mind to new perspectives and long-forgotten wisdom. Your insights are on fire. Join me, Moldavite, for the ride of your life. Five, four, three, two, one . . . blast off!

Affirmations

I rise up from any stressful situation better than I expect.

*I am ready to accelerate dramatic change and
release the truth.*

*I am connected to a long lineage of higher beings,
and I can tap into their energy anytime.*

MOONSTONE
The Cosmic Connector
Change, Mystery, and Balancing Cycles

I am Rainbow Moonstone, a potassium aluminum mineral of the orthoclase feldspar group, and I can hypnotize you with my beauty. I have a blue-white sheen caused by the presence of an optical phenomenon called adularescence. When you touch my smooth surface, you can feel my enchantment. In this image, I appear as a tall crystal point. You have chosen this card because you want to change your luck. I can help with that. Many believe a positive spirit inhabits me with the power to shift reality. I am also associated with the light of the Moon, and I can gently illuminate and balance different emotional and physical cycles. Put me under your pillow at night and don't be surprised if you fall into peaceful bliss. My hypnotic iridescent pearly sheen lulls you deep into my calming matrix, illuminating your feminine side and soul purpose. When using me, lucid dreaming and psychic abilities become enhanced, and you can safely uncover information about yourself that has eluded you in the past. I invite you to journey deep within your dark side. I will be there too—shining the light.

Joining our journey are a bear, a rabbit, a mockingbird,

moonflowers, the Full Moon, and Pluto. The powerful bear leans on me for support. He puts his paws together in acknowledgment of my wisdom. The bear only shows himself to fellow leaders—like you. He reminds you of your strength and your responsibilities. You must always lead with your heart, not your head. Old ways of ruling with an iron fist don't apply anymore. Helping and caring for people are what is important, and collaboration is key. The male mockingbird is one of the few birds that sings his song at night. He shares his vibrations with those who are asleep, desperately hoping to wake them. He says to maintain your boundaries and let nothing come into your space without your consent. This wisdom will protect you. He wants you to sing the song you came here to sing and know that with persistence you will be noticed. With the rabbit hopping around, you will always be productive and creative. But this is no ordinary rabbit—this is a goddess. She is shy, but she has come here to show you your extraordinary qualities (such as creativity, compassion, cooperation, tenderness, and intuition). The rabbit reminds you that you are here to inform the world (if not the universe) that the current masculine cycle we have been in for thousands of years has shifted. It is being replaced by the new divine feminine.

Moonflowers blossom in the dark and attract the most unusual pollinators. They teach you that beautiful things can flower in what seems to be impossible conditions. Moonflowers believe in romance and want you to let yourself enjoy being with another. You deserve to be loved! Pluto is here to show you that life will never be the same. Release anything that is weighing you down and allow yourself to move on. Epiphanies will sprout. When you hang around with me, Rainbow Moonstone, something divinely magical is just around the corner, hidden in plain sight. Perhaps stardom?

Affirmations

I stand up to anyone or anything that invades my space.

I easily connect with my higher wisdom, knowing I have all the answers.

I am able to connect with the divine feminine and feel compassion and love for all living things.

MYSTIC MERLINITE
The Magical Forgiver
Communication, Epiphanies, and Enchanted Memories

I am Mystic Merlinite, an igneous rock made up of feldspar, olverine, and quartz, and I can read your mind. I am also called Gabbro. I am a coarse-grained, black or dark-green stone found deep within the Earth's crust. I can awaken ancient memories that first set your personal patterns in motion. In this image, you can find me on the soft Persian carpet. You have chosen this card because you want to develop your supernatural abilities. Please work with me and my magic. What is a magical spell but the ability to manipulate reality with words? The word *abracadabra* literally means "as I speak, so I create!" The Egyptians believed in this. The following was found in the shrines of King Tut, "That the heavens and their hosts came into existence merely by pronouncing words whose sound alone evokes things. As its name is pronounced, so the thing comes into being. For the name is a reality; the thing itself." You may not have realized how heavy your thoughts have been or how light you will feel when you transform them. I help by stimulating your intuitive, clairvoyant, and psychic abilities. New timelines form from these epiphanies. The dark and light patterns that form in my stone remind you that you have both a light spiritual side and a dark shadow side—they are both equally important for your evolution.

Joining our journey are a lynx, a squirrel, two kestrels, a Persian rug, Mars, Neptune, two ancient trees, the Moon, and stars. A galactic party has started, and you are invited. It is exploding with exciting quantum power and new paradigms. The planets are revealing their esoteric knowledge: Neptune, the big blue planet, turns on your imagination; Mars, the red planet, stimulates your chakras; the Moon's light uncovers buried secrets; and the twinkling colorful stars illuminate your path. Portals are opening, and you are learning the language of quantum synchronicity. You will experience journeys to places you never dreamed of. This party brings you to the intersection of two timelines or two dimensions. Which way will you go? The choice is up to you. Will it be the way of the past, with old traditions and beliefs, and playing it safe, or will you shed all the old knowledge and embrace what is happening at this party? The lynx says to believe in yourself and your special abilities. Its distinctive ear tufts act as antennae allowing it to access the divine. Just tune in to their frequency to hear your Higher Self. The squirrel's behavior teaches you never to give up—if you don't succeed the first time, try, try again and again and again and again. And with the squirrel as your mentor, be ready to change directions in an instant. The kestrels' advice is the same—change, adapt, and recover.

You can gracefully rise above all the outside distractive cacophonies and find peace in knowing you are part of something much greater than yourself. The rug is a metaphor for how you feel about yourself. Do you let people walk all over you? Or do you know how enchanting and rare you are? The wise ancient trees are examples of living archaeology. They are rooted in the ground (stability) and grow toward the light (the universe)—a metaphor you need to embrace. These wise beings connect you to your soul home: the Earth and sky. Carl Sagan knew this when he said, "The cosmos is within us. We are made of star-stuff. We are a way for the universe to know itself." Everyone is invited to this cosmic party; the ticket of admission is to be the star you are. Let me, Mystic Merlinite, help you forgive yourself (and others) by synchronizing your heart and mind. The heart knows no judgment; it only welcomes harmony and love.

Affirmations

*I am a luminary, lighting the way
for others.*

*Without the darkness, I would never
see the stars.*

*I am a magical being who can tap into divine
energy whenever I want.*

OBSIDIAN
The Trauma Dissolver
Integration, Protection, and Truth Seeker

I am Black Obsidian, a piece of volcanic glass, and I will tell you the truth. I am born from extreme pressure, explosive energy, and magma erupting from a volcano. My edges are so hard, sharp, and naturally angular that the Native Americans often used me to make tools such as arrowheads, spearheads, knives, scrapers, and drills. I won't hold back anything! You have chosen this card because you are confused and want to know the truth. I can help. I bring clarity to your mind by being a mirror and reflecting back on your reality as objectively as I can. My razor-sharp edges dissolve emotional blockages and ancient traumas. And my black color encourages you to confront and integrate your dark, shadow side. When you embrace this mysterious ally, you become stronger and more able to fend off the constant mental, emotional, and spiritual attacks you experience daily. Wear me as jewelry or hold me and I energetically shield and protect you from negativity. I do this by forming a grounding cord that goes from your base chakra to the Earth's center. I am here for you; you are not alone.

Joining our journey are an American Eskimo dog named Dakota, Neptune, two Chilean volcanos and their landscapes

(Villarrica and Osorno), two Canada geese, and a pasque wild-flower. This piece is all about your personal evolution and transformation. You are going through challenging times, but you will prevail. Your faithful and protective dog, Dakota, is brilliant and will work for you day and night. Because he is naturally wary of strangers (he barks at them a lot!) he makes a great watchdog and protector. The two volcanos want you to remain balanced. They say to keep calm, take deep breaths, and make sure you don't let things build up inside of you. Wake up all that "sleeping energy" that you have buried deep within you and let it flow up and out. Constructive ways to release that pressure are journaling, meditating, exercising, or talking with a close friend.

Wildflowers are a bit mysterious because they just seem to pop up in the most unusual places. They are usually hearty plants that can thrive in even challenging conditions. Flowers like the pasque wildflower are called such because they don't need humans to propagate; they do it on their own—just some Sun, water, and space are all they need. Their message is to be as independent as you can, and you will grow and prosper. Relying on others too much can limit you. It is nice to interact and work with others, but remember to be true to yourself. Always remember to see all the beauty and abundance that surrounds you. Neptune spins magic into your life and connects you with your imagination, dreams, and spiritual visions. When it shows up in your life, expect your higher awareness and psychic insights to strengthen. The Canada geese want you to be free, but remember where you came from. These beauties mate for life. They are devoted to their family and are known for their loud "honking" and scaring predators away. Let me, Black Obsidian, Dakota, and the geese help you be brave and challenge anything that endangers you, your family, and your world.

Affirmations

I am as free as my mind allows me to be.

I feel a strong connection with Source and feel its protection and love.

I embrace my natural progression as a heart-based human and release that which no longer serves me or the planet.

PEARL
The Prosperous Learner
Respect, Prestige, and Self-Control

I am Pearl, composed of calcium carbonate (mainly aragonite and calcite), and I bring respect and prestige into your life. I am not actually a stone, but I am still considered a gem. In this image, I am balanced on the head of the baby giraffe and in the background. You have chosen this card because you need to develop self-worth. Interestingly enough, I also come from humble beginnings. I start as a grain of sand that finds its way into a species of mollusk. As a defense mechanism, the mollusk secretes a fluid to coat me. Layer upon layer builds up until I look like I do in this image—lustrous and radiant. Some think me an intruder, an irritant, but sometimes you must go through annoying life lessons to evolve into something extraordinary. This process has made me a symbol of wisdom gained through experience. Maybe this is why I have become a silent uniform of sorts for strong and powerful women. You play a more significant role in the theater of life than you realize. When you perform here with total abandon and passion (and learn to honor and understand your emotions), you can easily attract the prosperity you so want. Wearing me will also help you have more self-control, patience, and a heart-based view of life.

Joining our journey are a family of giraffes, two red roses, two dragonflies, two butterflies, a Full Moon, and a tall building. Giraffes are affectionate, gentle, and visionary creatures. Their long necks allow them to connect with the heavens while their feet stay firmly planted on the ground. Their advice is to gain a higher perspective before making any major decisions. See the big picture and don't get lost in small details. I enjoy balancing on the little giraffe's crown chakra. This position creates a spiritual connection with Source (God, Higher Self, etc.), reminding you that you have loving galactic parents. Since no two giraffes have the same patterns, they teach you to embrace what makes you—you! Oscar Wilde said it best, "Be yourself; everyone else is already taken!" The two roses held by the adult giraffes signify a deep love for family. They teach you that when you stay connected with your family (and community), you grow in emotional strength and well-being. The two dragonflies have the ability to see their world from different angles. They allow you to see through life's illusions and trust your natural intuitive abilities. Do not limit yourself; try new techniques and ideologies when dealing with any challenging situation.

Two butterflies (one blue and one orange—complementary colors) are attracted to my light. I believe these delicate beings have the ability to cross the veil between this dimension and the next. That's why they are popularly thought to symbolize change, rebirth, and even a person's essence or soul. These two butterflies are soulmates because they complement each other so well. When butterflies appear in your life, be prepared for a gradual but steady change. Stand firm and tall (like the building) during the process and know that I, Pearl, and the Full Moon will guide you to the light of status and success.

Affirmations

I have fun with my friends and family and draw strength from their love.

I am more beautiful than I realize, and I radiate this beauty out to the world.

Now is the time to connect with my Higher Self and let it elevate my consciousness.

PYRITE
The Creativity Unblocker
Energy, Willpower, and Encouraging Prosperity

I am Pyrite, an iron sulfide mineral, and I create sparks. My name comes from the Greek word *pyr,* which means "fire." My shiny yellow crystals have misled people into thinking I am gold (hence my nickname "Fool's Gold"). But don't you be fooled; I am still valuable. In fact, scientists have recently found that I actually do have a kind of gold within my structure that is easy to extract (ha-ha, fooled everyone). In this image, I am seated on either side of the pathway. You have chosen this card because you need a good boost. I can help with that. Hold a piece of me near your stomach (solar plexus chakra) and feel revitalized. This is because I stimulate cell regeneration. I also help restore and strengthen your memory. Meditate with me and feel my fiery energy burn away any fears and doubts you may have. It is my job to protect you from unbalanced energies, keep you healthy, and promote your happiness. Stay strong in your resolve to follow your passions. You are special—together we can accomplish and succeed at anything!

Joining our journey are a mitochondrion, two pyrite crystals, two peace lilies, a velvet worm, Jupiter, and Mars. The mitochondrion is teeming with cosmic energy. It is actually an energy portal. It represents a new understanding of quantum energy that will shift life as you know it. This applies to your health as well. Be selective with what you eat and exercise regularly; research the latest health information. The two pyrite crystals give you the strength and willpower to succeed while you evolve and transform. They also advise you to "do your homework" when making important decisions. You are more valuable than you realize. Two white peace lilies balance on either side of the mitochondrion. They come with a beautiful message of tranquility and neutrality. Remember to stay centered during stressful times and find positive ways of relaxing. Also, since NASA has proven it to be one of the best natural air purifiers, this might mean that you need to clean your home and work space. Make sure you are breathing clean air (you might need to buy a peace lily and/or an air purifier). Since two is the number of partnerships, diplomacy, and stability, chances are you will be working and/or living with another person who will bring peace and security to your life. There are ten leaves—five on either side. Ten is the number of leadership, but also of higher purpose. Something new is about to take place in your life. It may be associated with your ancestors, current family, or possibly future family. Seize any opportunity.

The velvet worm doesn't have a backbone, but it says you do! Maybe it is time you stood up to something you have backed away from. On the other hand, perhaps it is time to back down, chill, and let something go. Like the velvet worm, you might naturally be drawn to the beauty of the night. When others go to sleep, you are able to relax. Your creativity flourishes when uninterrupted. Also, the velvet worm wants you to know that no matter how alone you might feel, there are always others around you who feel the same. Jupiter is looking out for you with its positive message of expansion, success, good luck, and abundance. And Mars will bring you passion, courage, and the power to change the world for the highest and best good. Remember to work with me, Pyrite, and anything you touch will turn to gold!

Affirmations

My determination is unbreakable;
I am on fire!

Having a sense of humor is the best way
to stay healthy.

I can easily accomplish any or all of my goals,
wishes, dreams, and passions.

ROSE QUARTZ
The Nurturing Supporter
Empathetic, Nurturing, and Universal Love

I am Rose Quartz, a form of pink quartz also known as hyaline quartz, and I unconditionally love you. Microscopic minerals give my rosy pink color a clouded, milky translucent appearance. My smooth glassy luster will be hard to down! I am the stone of motherly, platonic, self, and universal love. I connect with feminine energy-enhancing compassion, nurturing, and empathy. In this image, I am perched atop two tall structures on either side of the Full Moon. You have chosen this card because you need to learn how to repair your sad, exhausted, and/or grieving heart. I can help by purifying and opening this divine gateway. A healthy heart fosters trust, harmonious relationships, and self-love. Keep me near whenever you need a calming, peaceful sensory experience and when you interact with groups of people. I will ensure you speak from your heart. I will envelop you in a frequency field of loving tenderness. It is said that I am quite effective in attracting new love, romance, and intimacy. I will work hard to dispel any negativity that surrounds you and even protect you against environmental pollution. And my beautiful pink color encourages you to express your creative passions by stimulating your imagination. In this image, I am perched high up for a better view of the situation.

Joining our journey are a peregrine falcon, two mocking-birds, two fish, five cows, grass, holy water, a trough, vines, music, butterflies, a fairy, the Flower of Life symbol, the Sun, and the Full Moon. The vines say when the whirlwind of activity swells up, and you feel you are about to blow away, hold on to them. They will activate your determination and strength. The solid, stable, grounded cows show you how to stay calm in dire cir-cumstances. Think of them standing together quietly, being one with the landscape. The falcon carries you up into your highest dreams, showing you how to rise above all situations. This solar bird makes sure that nothing trespasses too close to your creative and spiritual "eggs." The mockingbirds teach you how to com-mand peoples' attention with your voice. They advise you to think before you speak and then only speak from the heart/mind. The Full Moon wants you to live your life to the fullest—but be an example of sacred neutrality. Don't get frazzled by small chal-lenges, and take time to reflect. Fish wisdom is about smooth, gentle, beautiful change. They remind you that spiritual evolu-tion is your birthright. Remember, what you resist, persists.

Water is necessary for all life; before drinking it project posi-tive, compassionate, and forgiving intentions into it. It will fill your body with delightful vibrations. The Earth, fairy, and butterflies focus on whimsical and transformational energy. They say that it's time to sing your song and compose that powerfully emotional sym-phony. Tall grass is all about seeing the fresh, new, "radical" growth and evolution taking place in your life. Grass brings the promise of shifting old ways of dualistic thinking to new heart path wisdom. There is only *One* divine plan, and the Flower of Life is actually Source's (God's) shorthand. All consciousness as we know it arrives from this symbol. Know that you are part of the miracle of life and here to ensure its continuance. The light of the Sun says "know thy-self" and illuminates your truth. I, Rose Quartz, say—love yourself. Rupi Kaur, the Canadian poet, wrote, "How you love yourself is how you teach others to love you." Let me lead you to the cosmic trough and show you how to drink up all the love in the universe!

Affirmations

Magic surrounds me and illuminates latent powerful creative energy.

Abundance and prosperity are a state of mind; I go with the flow and allow it in.

I can travel the world, but my heart is the only place I find true beauty, peace, and love.

RUBY
The Enlightened Activator
Chi, Concentration, and Eternal Love

I am Star Ruby, a pinkish-red variety of the mineral corundum (aluminum oxide), and I increase your chi. My six-pointed star is created when tiny fibers of rutile, also known as silk, reflect light in such a way that I twinkle. This sparkling energy awakens your base chakra and improves your circulation. In this image, I hang from a botanical necklace. You have chosen this card because you want to be a better version of yourself. I can help you concentrate, enhance your self-confidence, and become downright invincible. Together we will create a new energetic template, allowing you to step out of your old limiting ways and into a new bio-suit (body). You will look the same; you will know that you have been upgraded. I will also help you with self-love. I bring light to your darkness and trigger an awakening of a part of yourself that you have suppressed in order to function in this world. If you carry trauma around with you (and who doesn't?), I will talk to your inner child. I will remind you that you are not your body and your soul can never be harmed. If you find yourself exhausted because you are looping in a cycle of overwork and not enough rest, I help break that pattern. Because of my deep sensual red color, I have always been considered a stone of the heart and love—not just any love, but a strong, powerful, and committed love. Wearing me will align with the frequencies of passionate, faithful, and eternal love. If you are looking for a special mate or close confidant, I will point you in the right direction. Not surprisingly, I also activate your kundalini energy. You may find that your creativity increases, and new ideas and ways of perceiving the world pour out of you.

Joining our journey are the ball python, desert rose, rose butterfly, fleur-de-lis, honeybees, Mars, Mercury, and the Sun. I have paired up with the ball python because it is a transformational creature: the shedding of its old skin reveals the new. Like me, it awakens your kundalini. Kundalini is your creative life force energy and consciousness, which has been coiled at the base of your spine since birth. As you spiritually evolve, energy is slowly released, triggering more life changes. If you see a snake, it means that your creative energies are awakening and that you are being initiated into a new belief system. Snake wisdom filters out that which is an illusion and helps you to see false beliefs that have been imposed on you since birth (and even earlier).

The huge Sun sheds light on the matrix's agenda. The matrix taps into the hive mind and controls reality by keeping us all looping in fear and illusion. The technique it uses is what I call magical thinking. Once you realize this is happening, you awaken from a deep sleep, and by the laws of physics, you attract the truth. The original design of the fleur-de-lis originated in ancient Egypt. It represented an asp. In this image, it signifies luxury and success. Mars is here to give you a big push to face your dark side. Layers and layers of clouds will dissipate, and you will see clearly for the first time. The butterflies are ready to assist you with your complete makeover. Your desert rose gives you the passion, strength, and love to see this new stage of your life blossom. And with Mercury close by, you will have a lot to talk about. I, Star Ruby, am ready for it. Now, wake the snake up!

Affirmations

I am a new, improved, and better version of myself.

*I wake up to my true birthright and claim
my authority and power.*

*Out with the old and in with new transformative
and loving energy.*

SEPTARIAN
The Boundary Maker
Honorable, Space, and Harmonious Vibrations

I am Septarian, composed of calcite, aragonite, barite, and limestone, and I protect and defend your honor. I am a unique mixture of rock, mineral, and organic matter. In fact, I am the result of volcanic activity from the Cretaceous period. My nodules (aka concretions) are formed from fossilized mud bubbles that are trapped, sealed, and dried under extreme pressure. This process creates a type of cement that looks like scaly skin patterns. Maybe that is why I am also called the Dragon Stone. In this image, I am standing to the right of an open door in a small room. You have chosen this card because you need your space. I am a natural at doing that. The word *septarian* comes from the Latin word *septum,* meaning "partition." My nodules contain angular cavities due to cracking, which are called septaria and create divisions throughout me. My advice to you is to create a special space to do your work and create. This could be a corner of a small apartment, a room in a house, or a studio/office in another building. "When you are alone, you are all your own," to quote Leonardo da Vinci. Having your own private space will give you the time to reboot. You still need to socialize— but you must take care of yourself first before dealing with others. Being associated with the dragon, I bring you the vibrations of confidence, bravery, power, and good fortune. I also nurture and protect you by grounding you to the Earth's frequency. Keep me nearby and feel my uplifting and harmonious vibrations surround you and bring balance back to your life.

Joining our journey are a pair of Emden geese, three golden eggs, a tickseed wildflower, a ladybug, a *junk* boat, the Gibbous Moon, and the Sun. The geese want you to make decisions for yourself. You mustn't automatically agree with others; listen to your inner voice and/or muse. Don't feed the *egregore* (the group mind)—it is a subtle force more controlling than you understand. Geese mate for life. Perhaps your current relationship is stronger than you think, or someone new could be waiting on the other side of the open door. Your three golden eggs symbolize new life, potential, and wealth. Like the golden eggs in Aesop's Fables, be careful that you don't undervalue something you own. This doesn't have to be material; it could be a talent you have or someone close to you. Be careful when cleaning and giving things away, for you may inadvertently throw something out that is more important than you realize. These special eggs want to know what new projects you are hatching right now. What three would you most like to focus on?

The wildflowers' wisdom is about being free and staying true to yourself. Keep life simple: you don't need much, just some food (support), water (renewal), and the Sun (passion). The Moon and iris (in the center of the wildflower) allow the light of truth, freedom, and nonconformity into your consciousness. The ladybug's advice is to know that size has nothing to do with power—you have more clout than you understand. The boat awakens the need to journey to real and imagined places. So don't be afraid to take risks; venture where your heart steers you. Take me, Septarian, and my components aragonite (stability), calcite (self-esteem), and limestone (grounding) along to ensure an egg-ceptionally fantastic voyage.

Affirmations

I bravely take the first steps toward a new optimistic world and a brilliant life.

I move confidently in the direction of my dreams, knowing I have the wind at my back.

I have my personal dragon watching out for me, sending me energy, strength, and protection.

SERPENTINE
The Time Traveler
Awakening, Stabilizing, and Clearing Past Traumas

I am Serpentine, a magnesium silicate mineral composed from lizardite, chrysotile, and antigorite, and I balance you. I am named for my wavy, fibrous, and scaly appearance—like a snake. My green color can be confused with jade, but on closer inspection, I am quite different. In this image, I appear at the bottom of a rhombus portal. You have chosen this card because you want to bring control back into your life. I can help with this. How? I can clear away your incessant mind chatter and negative thinking associated with past traumas. I also stabilize and invigorate your chakras, especially the crown chakra, encouraging spiritual awareness and psychic abilities. Work with me every day (especially holding me during meditation) and I will help you voyage deeply into your past lives. This practice helps you gain a deeper understanding of your many experiences and the roles you play in them. I help draw the Earth's energy up into your body, stimulating an awakening of long-dormant kundalini energy. What is kundalini? It is an energy that rests like a coiled serpent at the base of your spine, waiting for you to turn it on and remember how powerful you are. Once activated, you go through an energetic upgrade, which can be quite dramatic. But with me helping, you will connect with waves of blissfulness and see life through a new 5D lens.

Joining our journey are a pine marten, two hummingbirds, a four-leaf clover, a zebra primrose flower, four ladybugs, an ancient castle, the Full Moon, and the Sun. The pine marten shows up when you need to set boundaries, have more confidence, and turn on your magnetic personality. It is an independent critter that prefers its own company. If you feel like the marten, look for that special haven you can retreat to—like a park with trees (martens just love to be around the energy of trees). The hummingbirds want you to enjoy your daily routine and learn how to embrace happiness. Their motto is "don't take anything too seriously." The four-leaf clover and ladybugs bring you love, protection, and luck. They want you to have faith and hope, knowing that you are rare and special. And if there is someone in your life you can't live without, give them primroses. It means you want to live a full and happy life with them. The Full Moon is revealing new personal truths. This inner guidance will shift your perceptions and reality. It says: "I'll believe it when I see it," is not accurate. It is the other way around: "I'll see it when I believe it."

Quantum physics is asking you to reconsider some fundamental long-unexamined assumptions you learned in school and reinforced in the world—things such as linear time. Maybe time travel is possible; it's all how you perceive it. The past, present, and future as we know it are all happening simultaneously (you can experience it with what I call spherical thinking). Remember, just go with the flow and enjoy the present moment. That's where the Sun is rising, and the birds are singing. Share your story—it might be more critical to the future than you realize. Myths and legends from the past live on because we remember them and pass them down to our children. Journey with me, Serpentine, and create a new blueprint where you are healthy, happy, and celebrated. How exciting to be your own legend! But remember what Victor Hugo said, "If you don't build castles in the air, you won't build anything on the ground."

Affirmations

I am successful and I embrace my good fortune.

My body is waking up to new knowledge and wisdom.

I am ready to heal past unconscious traumas and be happy.

SMOKY QUARTZ
The Astral Protector
Powerful, Transmuting, and Answering Prayers

I am Smoky Quartz, a brownish-gray, translucent member of the common quartz family (silicon dioxide), and I work hard for you. My color is produced by natural radiation from surroundings rocks. The druids called me the "Stone of Power." And they were correct. My energy comes directly from Source, allowing me to connect with the upper and lower spirit worlds. In this image, I stand on top of the staircase in front of the opened doors. You have chosen this card because you need a champion to stand guard over you. I can do that since my job here on Earth is to keep you safe and grounded 24/7! How do I accomplish this? I surround you with an energetic protective shield. This not only keeps out any lingering negative energies but helps transmute them into something more positive. I am called Smoky Quartz because I capture the essence of billowing wispy smoke. Smoke rituals are used as a form of communication, answering prayers, and releasing earthbound souls. Hold me close to your heart when you want to contact departed loved ones and know they are safe. My association with the root chakra helps soothe your worries and allows you to feel protected. I also help to lessen tension, nervous energy, anxiety, and/or panic attacks. Meditate with me (face me downward) and release this energy into Mother Earth. When you are done, don't forget to sage or wash me.

Joining our journey are an ocellated turkey, three turkey eggs, Adam and Eve, an apple, three pansies, two acorns, the Full Moon, light language, and an entrance to another dimension. People think the color of a turkey is brown—but what has appeared here is a turkey that looks like it's part peacock. This beautiful bird has appeared in your painting to tell you that you can't always tell a book by its cover. What seems ordinary might just be really special. Turkeys in general are small, but this one is quite big. When you are ready to stand out and strut your stuff, call on the prosperous turkey. You may need to make some small sacrifices, but they will be well worth it. The eggs (creative dreams) have manifested and are ascending the steps. With your talent and passion, you will too! The fertile acorns and pansies hovering above show you that you can push through adversity and not only survive, but thrive. Remember, big things grow from little things. The pansies want you to think things through before making any important decisions. That is because the word *pansy* comes from the French verb *penser,* meaning "to think" or "to ponder."

The Full Moon sheds light on information that is hidden. For example, many believe that the biblical apple and Eve (representing all women) are bad. But some scholars believe this paradisiacal story has been mistranslated over the centuries. Paradise was not a heavenly place, but an enclosed, zoo-like structure. I believe that if someone was a specimen trapped in a zoo, he or she would question it. The two seated figures, Adam and Eve, are saying no to all past misinformation. For you, this symbolizes letting go of any old beliefs and negative personal agendas that keep you locked up— and allowing the hands of Source (truth) to support you. And just so you know, the proverbial apple's message is positive; it means sustenance and love. Let me, Smoky Quartz, interpret the light language from Source (written on the Romanesque-style tympanum framing the doorway/portal): "You are not alone. We are here to help, heal, and assist you in shifting your current world to one of peace and unity."

Affirmations

*I trust that all will be provided
as I need it.*

*I am stronger than I realize; nothing
can touch me.*

*Creativity is bursting from my soul; I overflow
with fertile ideas.*

STIBNITE
The Explosive Transformer
Programming, Reborn, and Explosive Power

I am Stibnite, a sulfide mineral sometimes called antimony, and I shake you up. I have a brilliant metallic luster and a lead to steel-gray color. I was born long ago when dinosaurs walked the Earth and volcanoes ruled the landscape. In this image, I appear in the nighttime sky and radiate in all directions. You have chosen this card because you want to be reborn. My knifelike crystals radiate out in all directions, cutting away the old to make way for the new. I am known to be a stone of Pluto, the planet associated with explosive power and "revolution." So, you can see how I would be linked with intense inner transformation. When you keep me within your sphere, you align with Pluto's dynamism (death and rebirth) and my healing frequencies. I was even used as medication in some ancient cultures. If you want to peel off old layers of outdated belief systems and tap into your original programming, I am the stone to carry around. Keep me close when writing and reciting affirmations (the secret to shifting your reality) and see synchronicities increase. Combine me with moldavite, and together we will blast open your heart and clear any negativity you have picked up in the past.

Joining our journey are a blue rose, a luna moth, two ladybirds, Mt. Fuji, Pluto, three seals, a sea lion, and a dolphin. The dolphin is in a dimension all its own. It has come to remind you to focus on being positive. It knows that laughing is healthy. This quotation by Dr. Madan Kataria says it all. "I have not seen anyone dying of laughter, but I know millions who are dying because they are not laughing." Laughter has a way of improving your health by decreasing stress hormones and increasing infection-fighting antibodies. It triggers the release of endorphins, the body's natural feel-good chemicals, that can even temporarily relieve pain. And all this is free, unlike doctors! Remember, happiness is a choice. It comes from inside—never from others. When you exude positivity, you attract others with the same energy. You have to be it to attract it— the same with love.

With Mt. Fuji, Pluto, and I appearing together, expect things in your life to change. Although it might be hard to see at first, change is for the better—no matter how intense. Any birthing brings drama, but eventually things settle down—and when they do, you will see you're in a much better place than before. You are moving into a different kind of reality in which your assumptions about the nature of physical objects, time, and space will no longer be what you are used to. The moth and seals say to be brave, go inside, uncover mysteries, and go toward the light. Trust your intuition more than anything you read or hear on the news or others. The sea lion sleeps twelve hours a day. It wants to help you improve your sleep habits. Are you getting eight hours of sleep a night? Be honest! If you are going to change the world, you need to rest. What will shift our planet? It will not be the "chosen ones," shamans, and/or sages—it will be you, your friends, and your family. We have the power. We are all receiving upgrades in the form of synchronicities. When the blue rose blossoms, "miracles" will become the norm. We will succeed because the ladybirds vibrate prosperity, abundance, and success. Follow me, Stibnite, to a world (and timeline) that explodes with new possibilities and promises love.

Affirmations

Every time I laugh, I get a facelift.

*I am a powerful force here to shift
the planet.*

*I tap into my original programming and
connect with my ancient creators.*

SUGILITE
The Devotional Shielder
Uplifting, Supernatural, and Universal Healing

I am Sugilite, a sodium-potassium lithium iron aluminum silicate mineral, and I share your heart. I am a rare mineral that is best known for my vibrant pink to purple colors. But I also come in light brownish yellow, reddish violet, and colorless. My beautiful purplish color comes from small amounts of manganese. In this image, I manifest in the shape of a heart. You have chosen this card because you want to uplift your body and soul with divine love. I can help with that. Purple is a charismatic color associated with intuition, creativity, and spirituality. Hold me in your hands, close your eyes, and visualize you are connected to your Higher Self (or Source, God, Angels, etc.). Allow yourself to experience this universal healing love. If you are suffering from any dis-ease, chances are you need to allow more love and light into your consciousness. I will help you with this by balancing your nervous system and letting go of unnecessary fears and tensions. When your mind is calm, you allow the wisdom of your bio-suit (body) to take over. Put me under your pillow at night if you have difficulty slowing down. I can help you release unwanted and annoying energies that you picked up during your busy day. See my protective energetic shield of love amplify your ambitions and dreams. I also connect you with your ancestors on the other side of the veil. This energetic portal is always available to you with the right frequency key—which I have!

Joining our journey are two emperor penguins, two blue jays, three zebra fish, five starfish, two sprigs of gladiolus, Jupiter, and ACTH molecules. Humanity is in the midst of a profound transition. The way we decode reality is very interesting. It isn't what we think it is—nothing is. You are in the process of changing who you are, where you live, how you live, and the very foundational principles on which you base your existence. You reject the old "normal," which no longer resonates with you. Your Higher Self says you have skills and abilities at your fingertips, that (with a little tweaking and updating) will help shift the world. Because penguins are such deep divers, they symbolically connect you with different realms (like the astral/dream realm) that exist at higher vibrational frequencies. Imagine turning on an old radio and tuning in to WHUD on FM. What happened to all the other stations, such as AM and SIRIUS? Well, they are still playing. You just haven't turned to that station or frequency. Jupiter (the planet of expansion and good fortune) magnifies all the nearby energies, guaranteeing that all the signals will be loud and clear. When the boisterous blue jays show up, you know your distinctive voice and fashion sense will be noticed. Like the starfish, the zebra fish brings you the power to heal and regenerate. They say you can grow back anything you think you have lost. As long as you don't let the stress molecules (ACTH) take over, you will be fine. In Latin, *gladiolus* translates into "little sword," and your faithful, pink gladiolus will cut through anything that prevents you from connecting with your mother (whether here or on the other side of the veil). Let me, Sugilite, help you clear the clouds so you might find your true place in the universe. Yoko Ono said it well, "A dream you dream alone is only a dream. A dream you dream together is reality."

Affirmations

*I allow the forgiving purple ray of
light into my life.*

*I am here to help make the dream of love
a reality for the entire planet.*

*I don't have relationships with
people and things;
I have energy exchanges—
I exchange love.*

TANZANITE
The Compassionate Regenerator
Dazzling, Honesty, and Eternal Partnership

I am Tanzanite, a rare blue-violet variety of the mineral zoisite and part of the epidote mineral group, and I want to partner with you for life. Let me dazzle you with my very rare color characteristic known as trichroism. This effect happens when light causes three different colors to dance across my surface when viewed from three different directions. In this image, I appear as a ring floating in the stars. You have chosen this card because you want attention, devotion, honesty, and respect from a partner. I can help with that. When you wear me as an engagement ring, I symbolize new beginnings and hope for a bright future. And the gold in this ring enhances prosperity, love, and passion. The shape of a circle in general, stands for the eternal—no beginning and no end—like love. This ring is my pledge that we will be energetically connected as long as you desire. You will love that I vibrate at an amazingly high frequency and am associated with compassion, forgiveness, gratitude, and spiritual love. I am also known to support your immune system and improve your vitality. And my intense blue-violet color has been documented to lower blood pressure. This, in turn, helps calm your nerves and reduce stress.

Joining our journey are a violet plant, five hamsters, a male and female red-winged blackbird, four dragonflies, the Crescent Moon, the Sun, and the hands of Source. The doors open up to a space filled with light and love. Violets symbolize many things, some of which are innocence, modesty, and true love: love that lasts forever. I am not just talking about romantic love but also self-love and universal love. Because four dragonflies (balance, support, and organization) are landing on the violets (creativity, inspiration, and intuition), I believe you will be working on inspiring projects with others at home and/or at work. These transformational creatures are here to tell you that you're ready for a change, and that they are here to get you started. The five adventurous hamsters remind you that life can be fun and to find some friends to "play with." And they also believe that, although nothing is perfect, you should still strive to be the best you can be—and to take chances! Hikaru Nakamura is correct when she says, "In chess you try to do your best, but there are instances where you make mistakes or you try and take risks that you shouldn't. And I think losing games is a good thing, because you learn more from when you lose than when you win." Blackbirds are here to shift you to the next level of your "awakening." Even when you think you know a lot, they will surprise you with new esoteric information. You are ready to hear it! The Sun tells you that an old chapter of your life is ending, and a fresh new day is dawning. It is activating your divine blueprint and a productive time filled with growth and opportunities is at hand. Now is the time to take action.

A delicate Crescent Moon (duality, the feminine, and creativity) is on the top right of this image. If you look closely, you can see something called *Earthshine*. Earthshine is the dim glow on the darkened portion of the Moon. It is light from the Earth cast on the night side. This symbolically means that what was hidden in the past is gradually being exposed. No matter what is revealed, you need to realize that you are a child of the universe and you are safe.

Celebrate with me, Tanzanite, and the hands of Source, and know you are supported by divine love. Wake up to the best, most valuable day of your life . . . today!

Affirmations

I live life to the fullest and appreciate every moment.

I feel the eternal love of the Universe (Source) surrounding and protecting me.

Nothing is what it seems, and what I thought was a fact before is no longer certain.

TIGER'S EYE
The Courageous Gatekeeper
Opportunity, Willpower, and Primal Instincts

I am Tiger's Eye, a semiprecious variety of quartz, and I stand guard over you. I am a member of the chalcedony mineral family, known for my silky sheen. I am the gatekeeper of this dimension. In this image I hover above in the shape of a heart. You have chosen this card because you want to learn to be a shapeshifter. I can teach you how. Look at me closely, and you will see me transform before your eyes. My lustrous appearance is caused by tiny mineral crocidolite fibers dancing back and forth as they transform into silica. This mesmerizing effect results in sharp, parallel eyelike lines called chatoyant. But actually, all I am doing is connecting with the structure of the universe—also known as sacred geometry. You can learn to do this too. Just hold me as you visualize connecting with the universal matrix. This connection will shift you from a victim to someone of inner strength, self-confidence, and willpower. Use me as an amulet (like the Romans did), and I will activate my supernatural powers of protection—shielding you from things you think can hurt you. My name conjures up the powers of the tiger: strength, courage, and quick reflexes. It is a reminder of the importance of primal instincts and accepting your shadow side (that part of your personality you don't want to see or admit having).

Joining the journey are an Abyssinian cat (actually my cat

called Maya) and an iris stargate. Maya is peering out from the dimensional energy portal. She loves and encourages everyone to be brave and risk entering this transformative doorway. She is fearless and has often traveled back and forth to ancient Egypt. In fact, her lineage is the closest breed to the sacred cats of that time. Maya is very active, more active than most cats, and will always find something to amuse herself. She wants you to enjoy your own company as she does. This affectionate, alert, and intelligent cat loves to jump and play. She resonates with the energy of a kitten, no matter her age. Maya reminds you that there is no time. Linear time is just one of many limiting beliefs we hold on to. So let it go, step into the wormhole, and feel the rush of experiencing places you never dreamed of.

Presently, the concept of stargates exists only in the imaginations and minds of science fiction writers and theoretical astrophysicists; in this image, it is real. And as Einstein said, "Imagination is more important than knowledge. For knowledge is limited, whereas imagination embraces the entire world, stimulating progress, giving birth to evolution." It is time to experience true light and shift your perception of reality. Everything has prepared you for this moment. See yourself stepping through the threshold and experiencing personal and universal knowledge that helps you in this lifetime and others. Make this a daily practice, and you will be amazed at what your "imagination" creates. Once you experience the pure light of Source, you will never want to return home to the third dimension. Travel the galaxy with me, Tiger's Eye, and experience an indescribable bliss that's just purr-fect.

Affirmations

I am open to new and exciting experiences.

I am always in the right place at the right time!

Reality is just a collective hunch; it is not as it appears.

TOPAZ
The Stress Reliever
Relaxing, Successful, and Inner Vision

I am Blue Topaz, a silicate mineral made up of aluminum and fluorine, and I will recharge you. In my natural state I am colorless, but impurities can make me a pale blue, golden brown, and yellow orange. If you see me in any other colors (like my glacial blue), then I have been irradiated. In this image, small irregular-shaped pieces of me are scattered on the floor at the bottom of the image. You have chosen this card because you need to calm your mind. I can help with that. I evoke the soft blues of nature, allowing you to shift your mood. Hold on to me when you want to alleviate the day's stress. I do this by aligning your energy meridians. Also, place me under your pillow for a restful and tranquil night. When you wake, you will find you are better able to communicate your true feelings—and are a much more patient listener. Give me as a gift to someone special, and they will know how much you care for them. If you are an artist, I can clear your inner vision of annoying mental distractions allowing you easier access to creative insights and heightened perceptions of beauty. Because there are twenty pieces of me, your message is to have faith that special opportunities are manifesting in your life.

Joining our journey are a rabbit, a family of polar bears, a dove, two keys, two snakes, twelve human hands, the Full Moon, the

Earth, and the Sun. It is not surprising that the rabbit will jump-start your creativity. It wants you to believe that you can accomplish more than you think you can. You are a master at manifesting what you see in front of you all the time. It's a bit like *I Dream of Jeannie* or *Bewitched* (with the blink of an eye or the wiggle of a nose). They believed in their own powers—and that faith fueled their beliefs, perceptions, and abilities. When you trust, you will attract miracles! The dove has come to bring you peace of mind, support, and love. It's easy to be drawn into their hypnotic and soothing cooing, especially at dawn and dusk. Like me, the dove's compassionate, nonjudgmental energy can restore tranquility to those who have been traumatized. That's why it's a symbol of unconditional love. The dove views the world through a lens of warmth and caring. It stands strong, resisting negative forces.

The polar bear snuggles with its young. Its exterior is intimidating and powerful, but did you know it is a gentle and loving parent? The bear's message is to balance power and sensitivity. Stand up for what you believe in as long as you are centered in the heart. And the bear never gets lost because it attunes with the Earth's energy grid (similar to your inner meridians). You can always find your way home by listening to your body. The bear is also associated with both the Sun (your consciousness) and the Moon (your unconscious) due to its hibernating pattern. The Full Moon, hovering in the keyhole, says you have the resources to unlock the healing and intuitive abilities associated with your feminine side. It wants you to give a helping hand to people in your life that are in need. When you help others, you help yourself. Two snakes form the boundaries of a heart-shaped dimensional portal. Like the bear, they want to transform your life by awakening a part of you that has been asleep. As the snake sheds its skin, you must also let go of what is holding you back from your creative and spiritual destiny. Know that what you see right now is reality shifting in ways you never thought possible. You have the keys to unlock your dreams. Take a picture with me, Blue Topaz, and I will ensure you stay focused.

Affirmations

I relax and let go, and I share that feeling with others.

I accept that which needs to be released so that I may keep evolving.

It is time to stop and smell the roses—in fact, it is time to become the roses (love)!

TOURMALINE
The Universal Lover
Compassion, Heart, and Soothing Sensations

I am Pink Tourmaline, part of a complex family of aluminum borosilicates mixed with iron, magnesium, or other various metals, and I warm your heart. I am commonly found in a matrix of quartz. I come in more colors than any other gemstone: green, blue, yellow, pink, red, or colorless. Here, my pink color is due to the trace element manganese. In this image, I manifest as two cylinders being held by energetic hands. You have chosen this card because you want to take your understanding of love to a new level. I can help you with that. I am all about love: deep, deep, compassionate self-love, unconditional love, and emotional healing. I represent a kind of love that is so profound that it goes beyond that which you share in your human relationships—it reaches out to the universe! I am being offered to you by the hands of Source. If these times are causing you anxiety, keep me close by. I can reverse negative feelings and replace them with more positive and constructive alternatives. When you feel emotionally unbalanced, lie down and place a small piece of me over your heart. This allows my healing energies to be directly absorbed into your body. Also, place me under your pillow if you have trouble sleeping. My soothing vibrations calm your emotions and help you unwind.

Joining our journey are a water buffalo, a llama, an egret, four ladybugs, two ants, a heart, the Devil's Tower, the Full Moon, and ancient text. The large healthy heart at the top of the image beats life into your soul. Your soul and your heartbeat are entwined. Their mission is simple—to keep you healthy while living here on Gaia. How? Honor and respect your bio-suit by getting enough sleep, fluids, proper diet, exercise, and a dose of beauty. Relaxation is an art form—practice it. If you have anything that bothers—share it with me. The water buffalo reminds you to be kind and patient with friends and family. You are here to be of service to others—and you are good at it because you are a natural empath. The llamas are very focused on achieving their goals. They radiate resiliency and confidence. They honor who you are and what you do. The solitary egret helps you concentrate and look deeper into aspects of your life you have taken for granted. It wants you to know that you have what it takes to do the job—alone. But although each of the two ants has their own job, they need to cooperate—that is, if they want to succeed. The distinctive ladybugs lead you to success and good luck, and since there are four of them, you will certainly accomplish your dreams.

The Devil's Tower is considered a sacred space by Native Americans; it is the birthplace of wisdom. It was never associated with the devil—just a misinterpretation of the word *bear* (bad). In fact, this monolith symbolizes bear energy (kindhearted leadership). The ancient text (or light language) says to erase the old and allow a new birthing to take place. The Full Moon rising above the dense cloud layer shines a light on this next development. You are here to jump-start the collective heart at precisely the right moment by restoring its normal rhythm. I, Pink Tourmaline, and the entire universe are counting on you—no pressure!

Affirmations

*I am a channel for beings of love
and light.*

*I release any hidden programming and
welcome clarity.*

*When I connect with my heart, I hear the vibrations
and sounds of my true home.*

TURQUOISE
The Divine Purifier
Cleansing, Stabilizing, and Karmic Shifting

I am Turquoise, an opaque, hydrated copper aluminum phosphate mineral, and I cleanse you. My name comes from the French word *turqueise,* meaning "Turkish stone." I was also believed to be a stone of protection by the ancient Persians who called me *pirouzeh,* which translates to "victory." Today, my blue-green hue is so popular that a color has been named after me. In this image, I hover over a plant floating in a dimensional portal. You have chosen this card because you want to learn how to connect with healing energies from the cosmos. I am good at that. It is believed by many ancient cultures and spiritual shamans that I have the power to open up a conduit between this dimension and others. This allows me to access and gather specific information and procedures needed to heal the human body—similar to an energetic med-bed. If you have attracted unbalanced energies in the past, I can help you remove them from your emotional and physical environments. This allows your chakras to spin and your moods to stabilize. Thirteen pieces of me appear here set in gold. Thirteen is the number of renewal. It is a karmic shifter. Gold represents achievement, the divine, and generosity. Get ready to allow new positive ideas, people, and places into your life and heart!

Joining the journey are a hybrid human-dragonfly named

Claramond, a succulent plant, a snowy owl, an Asian leopard cat, twenty-one books, a strawberry, two blueberries, two ants, ladybugs, two oxygen molecules, and two batteries. Claramond is standing strong, accessing the loving energies from the batteries on either side of her. She has come from another dimension to deliver her message. Like her, you are something special and unique. Never underestimate how influential you are. People are drawn to you—without you even speaking a word! You are here to do spiritual surgery—and are good at it. The type of surgery you do is called spiritual reprogramming. It is what I am doing with you right now. You will never be the same because something inside of you has been activated and can never be turned off. You now have a clearer and brighter way of seeing reality (her dragonfly lineage teaches her to see things from another perspective). Your energy increases, your normal hearing expands, and all your senses become heightened. Clairaudience is turned on, and you can now hear and sense things you couldn't perceive in the past—like noticing your chakras spinning faster. Waves of blissful electrical pulsations move up and down your body. You understand how everything is one.

But your journey here is a challenging one. The succulent plant shows you that you can survive harsh and unfavorable conditions and still thrive. Your snowy owl is courageous and teaches you how to be a fierce but compassionate individual with the ability to cooperate with others. The cat brings you the courage and confidence to go deep within, accessing your intuition. It also teaches you to set loving boundaries. The twenty-one books are here to let you know you have started your spiritual journey and are being helped along the way. They represent all your interests, dreams, and passions. What new "books" will you be buying and putting on your shelf? The berries have the ability to manifest small blessings. But these seemingly minor blessings are magnified by the power of the batteries. The oxygen molecules connect you with Source's/God's breadth. Every breath is sacred. Breathe deeply and experience your true power. It is much more than you could ever imagine. I, Turquoise, want you to tap into the currents of the cosmos, knowing you can live your life like a magical fairy tale. The happy ending you always wanted is possible. I will cleanse you of any disbelief. Feel my unconditional love; follow the light of my heart—to spiritual and material good fortune and victory.

Affirmations

I am waking up and embracing the magic
and mystery of my life.

When I see my life situation from another angle,
I gain a more objective view.

I have my own personal dragonfly watching out for me,
sending me energy and strength.

VANADINITE
The Risk Taker
Adventurous, Daring, and Problem-Solver

I am Vanadinite, a lead vanadate chloride that belongs to the apatite group of minerals, and I help you take risks. I am used a great deal in industry (because of my vanadium and lead content), and usually come in bright red or orange-red colors, although there are times when I am more brown, red-brown, gray, yellow, or colorless. I am a dense, brittle mineral usually found in hexagonal crystals. In this image, I appear floating in a starry, hexagonal portal. I am called the mitochondria of the universe because my energy fuels your ability to produce. I love helping you with both serious work-related deadlines as well as fun, playful events. You have chosen this card because you want to be more adventurous. I can help you. My brilliant red color is both stimulating and calming at the same time. It gently nudges you out of complacency. Allow me to awaken dormant energies, giving you the creative boost needed to do what needs to be done. Step out of old routines and habits and dare to try something you have never done before. Keep me nearby when problem-solving and I will free your mind from confining societal structures and expectations. This allows you to find and access your original blueprint, or soul purpose, and understand how to interpret it. Because of my lead content, I am also helpful in protecting you against radiation in your environment—especially radiation caused by electronics such as your phones and computers.

Joining the journey are a female and male robin, six ants, four silkworms, Mercury, a tree, and a hexagonal portal. The devoted robin is a hard worker. Remember the expression the early bird catches the worm? Well, it was written about robins. These dependable and persistent birds are considered to be some of the best parents among all birds. They make sure that everyone is safe and well taken care of. When these birds catch your attention, it is time to see how your family is doing—and perhaps your neighborhood as well! The robins' message is to trust in your own abilities, be independent, and be confident. They want you to let go of anything that no longer serves you. Doing this frees you to move in new directions. The six-sided hexagonal opening symbolizes wisdom, love, and justice. And the six industrious ants strolling around the circle represent creation, perfection, and divine power. When ants show up in your life, the obvious symbolism is that you are part of a collective. Taking it further, you need to embrace teamwork, cooperation, and hard work to achieve your goals. They never give up! Four silkworms are spinning their silken cocoons around the hexagonal dimensional portal. Four is a steady, balanced number. The life cycle of the silkworm is a busy one and teaches you that what you want takes time and consistency. These selfless workers give life not only to future silkworms but allow others to create art and beauty with what they produce. Nothing is wasted. By eating a diet of mulberry leaves, they are able to spit out precious silk. You too need to eat a special diet to feel your best and be productive. It may feel like you are going in circles, but you are not. You are actually more stable than you realize. Mercury symbolizes the mind and communication. If Mercury has found its way to you, it might be because you are in a profession where you interview others, present information, or just enjoy communicating in general. This planet beckons you to be careful not to speak without thinking first. Be selective and sensitive when discussing topics that might alienate others. Also, let others have a chance to share their thoughts. You might just learn something valuable. The stable tree (between the chicks), reminds you that not everything is as it seems. It looks dead in the winter, but it is not! When the conditions are right, it will resurrect and be even stronger and more beautiful than before. Take a chance with me, Vanadinite, and remember, playing it safe is about the most dangerous thing you can do.

Affirmations

I easily change old habits into new successful ones.

I visualize my dreams and know they will come true.

Everything I have done up to this point has prepared me for what is to come.

GLOSSARY

Abracadabra

This term is most commonly associated with childhood games and magic shows, but its origin dates back hundreds of years to a time when people actually believed that the word *abracadabra* was a magical spell. The literal translation of this word is "I will create as I speak," from the Aramaic phrase *avra kehdabra*. Well, before one speaks, one experiences a thought. Combine thought and speech and you have an ancient formula for creative power. René Descartes (the French philosopher and scientist) took this a bit further with his famous statement, "I think therefore I am." In other words, this means "I come into existence because of my thoughts." The world around me is formed by my beliefs.

The word *abracadabra* was first recorded in a Latin medical poem by a Roman physician in the second century CE. This poem repeats the word continuously, forming an upside-down pyramid or funnel. Along with the poem are instructions stating that to help heal a sick person, you need to wear this repeated word around your neck like an amulet.

ACTH Molecules

ACTH is all about stress. It is a hormone made in the pituitary gland during times of anxiety. This hormone is released into the bloodstream several times a day in intermittent pulses. If you are feeling stressed, you are not alone—your body is feeling it with you. Stress means different things to different people. Our ancestors would have felt stress from a charging animal such as a lion. But today, most of us deal more with an aggressive boss or a screaming landlady. Stress is a mixed blessing. It's good if it motivates you, but bad if it wears you down. The more you are stressed, the more ACTH is released. ACTH stimulates the adrenal glands, which sit atop the kidneys, and they release two hormones called cortisol and adrenaline (also known as epinephrine). These hormones help you respond to stress in a healthy way and support your immune system.

Adularescence

If you love Moonstone, it is because of its special optical quality. Its smooth, milky bluish luster or radiance seems to lure you into the stone, just below its surface. The effect is called adularescence, and is also commonly referred to as the schiller effect. The schiller, appearing to move as the stone is turned, gives the impression of celestial light being caught in the stone. Another term for this effect is *sheen.* As opposed to luster, which is just on the surface of a polished gemstone, sheen originates below the surface and is caused by its interaction with light. Other stones with this characteristic are common opal, rose quartz, and agate.

Affirmation

If you speak or think any thought, you are basically creating an affirmation. The word is from the Old French *afermacion* ("confirmation") and from the Latin *affirmationem* ("to make steady," "to strengthen," or "to confirm"). Any time you speak you confirm—consciously and unconsciously—and it can be either negative or positive. My definition of an affirmation is a mindful thought or spoken intention in the present tense focusing on abundance, prosperity, and peace. Since thoughts and spoken words have frequencies, affirmations increase positive energy and help shift us out of negative states. If what we put our attention to becomes our reality, then it is important that we affirm this from the heart!

Akashic Records

If you have ever seen the comic movie *Defending Your Life* with Meryl Streep and Albert Brooks, you will understand what

Hollywood thinks the Akashic Record is—and its purpose. It is from the Sanskrit word *akasha,* meaning "sky," "space," "luminous," or "aether." The Akashic Records, also known as the Hall of Records or the collective unconsciousness, is not so much a literal place as it is a dimension, frequency, and/or life force. It is that "place" that determines our eternal human dramas and challenges. Some believe it exists in our DNA or on the astral plane or maybe it is even holographic. Since the human mind needs to put things in a visual language to make them more understandable, it tends to see the Akashic Records as a large library or temple. This library contains the soul's records of all its experiences in all of its lifetimes. Each soul has its own records that appear like a series of books, and each book represents one lifetime. In a nutshell, the Akashic Realm is an enormous storage system. It contains all the collective consciousness of our dreams, as well as our past, present, and future lifetimes. It records every thought, action, emotion, and experience that has ever happened in time and space in every lifetime. The purpose of the Akashic energy field is to learn and grow from the collective wisdom it stores. The record is nonjudgmental. It sees you with total and unconditional love and compassion. When you know something (an idea, a word, or a language) and don't know how you know it, chances are you paid a visit to the Akashic Records.

Aura

All living things have an aura. It is an energetic, luminous force field, so to speak, that surrounds your physical body. The aura is not just a halo around you, but is also an extension of your being and linked with your mind. Anything that affects the aura also does the same to your physical body and vice versa. Things such as what you eat or drink, sleep or lack of it, and stress can throw off the balance of energy in both your physical and etheric bodies, affecting your emotions. That is why your aura needs to be cleaned and cleared daily to rid it of energies that you have picked up that are not yours and need to be released. Doing this regularly ensures your well-being. See also *Energetic Field/Signature*.

Awakening

The dictionary definition of *awakening* is "an act or moment of becoming suddenly aware of something." As used in this book, *awakening* signifies becoming cognizant that we have been taught misinformation from childhood on up (by teachers, parents, and friends) in the name of control and conformity. For reasons unknown, there are forces that create situations that keep us all looping, questioning, and fighting. Once we learn the truth and "wake up," we see what has been perpetrated and know that nothing can ever have power over us again.

Bio-suit

Have you ever seen a sci-fi movie where the aliens wear a spacesuit that looks organic? Then when the suit is removed, it reveals the true alien form? This bio-suit allows them to survive in all extraterrestrial environments. It's similar to a spacesuit design we have that uses biomedical skin replacements and materials instead of conventional bulky suits (like a second skin approach). Well, I believe the human soul inhabits the body in a similar way. Our true form is energetic and we need this bio-suit in order to navigate life on Earth.

Cellular Memories

The concept of cellular memory has been part of human consciousness for centuries. It is the belief that the brain is not the only organ that remembers, stores, and recalls experiences. Rather, the body itself can hold on to old memories—even from past lifetimes. Science (and what science refers to as "pseudoscience") have been accusing each other of limiting information or intentionally misinforming. There are many theories about the body and cellular memory floating around. Some experiments have shown that individual cells and networks of non-neural cells possess something like cognition and can form memories. So, it is clear that brains and nerves are not the only possibilities for recording memory. The fact that so-called legitimate experiments have found that cells can consistently behave in unexpected ways tells us that cells do have a type of consciousness of their own. I believe when something is part of the collective consciousness—it exists. Time has shown me that we can't dream up or create what we don't already know—it has to come from some mechanism already in place.

Chakra System

Most people have heard about chakras and know they are in the body somewhere, but don't quite understand their functions. The name itself comes from the Sanskrit word meaning "wheel." Why was it called a wheel? Well, chakras are how energy moves through the front and back of the body. This "electrical" energy is affected by our emotional and physical experiences on Earth. Sometimes, like a wheel, it moves clockwise, spinning energy out of the body into the space around us, and sometimes it spins counterclockwise, pulling energy from our external world toward us. Somehow, ancient people knew that seven major areas spin around at different points along our spines. These multidimensional points correspond with bundles of nerves, major organs, and other important energetic areas. These are the names and locations of the chakras: root (at the base); sacral (just below the belly button); solar plexus (in the stomach area); throat (right at the throat); heart (near the heart); third eye (between your eyes); and crown (at the top of the head). As long as these energy disks stay open and spinning, you will remain mentally and physically healthy. If any of these points pulls negativity from the outside, the chakras could slow or even shut down. That is when you develop a physical, emotional, and/or spiritual problem. Focusing on your breath, meditation, doing specific yoga exercises, sound healing, and visualization can help bring these energy centers back into balance.

Channel/Channeling

A channel is a person, and channeling is what they do. They are often called shamans, witch doctors, prophets, psychics, and mediums. Most are searching for wisdom, the nature of consciousness, spiritual truths, and higher planes of reality, among other things. These people are able to act as antennas, picking up frequencies they believe are given off by nonphysical beings (often with the help of spirit guides) such as those who have passed, entities, spirits, aliens, star systems, and even God. Channeling is neither positive nor negative; it is just extrasensory sensitivity. We all have the ability to quiet ourselves down and sense different energies. It is quite normal that we all have some ability on the channeling spectrum. Like anything else, the more you focus on it, the stronger it gets. But to channel, you need to learn how to shift your mind and mental perceptions in order to attract and connect to this expanded state of consciousness. It has been proven that meditating helps shift brain waves and tunes in to a higher state of consciousness. Before embarking on any new spiritual adventure, always protect yourself by connecting with your heart and asking for the highest and best good.

Chatoyant

When you pick up a piece of tiger's eye, it is hard not to notice its visual poetry. As you turn it slightly to the left or right, it displays a vertical light dancing across its surface. *Chatoyancy* is the name given to this beautiful optical effect. It occurs in stones that contain a large number of very thin parallel inclusions within the stone, known as silk. The light reflects from these inclusions to form a thin band across the surface of the stone. The band of light always occurs at right angles to the length of the parallel inclusions. If you own a cat, you will understand why this phenomenon is called the cat's eye effect. Stones that display this trait are tourmaline, apatite, beryl, actinolite, demantoid garnet, scapolite, sillimanite, and quartz, among others, but only chrysoberyl can be called simply cat's eye or tiger's eye quartz.

Chi

You can thank chi energy for being alive. The Chinese were one of many ancient peoples to notice it and give it a name. Simply put, chi (qi) is a vital life force that powers all living organisms. It is akin to the fuel in your car or electricity going into batteries when you charge them. It is the essence of existence that flows through each of us, uniting the body, mind, and spirit. It needs to be honored, respected, and maintained. If you abuse your body in any way, you deplete your chi, resulting in low energy and/or disease. Some ways you can increase chi are with a balanced diet, adequate sleep, stretching the body, and acupuncture.

Clairaudience

If you have ever heard a persistent voice in your head giving you advice (most times protecting you), then you have experienced some type of clairaudience. It is one of many "clairs," three of them being claircognition, clairvoyance, and clairsentience. Clairaudience is the psychic sense of hearing. It comes from the French-Latin roots *clair* ("clear") and *audientia* ("hearing"), meaning "a clear sense of hearing." This extrasensory talent can be experienced in different ways. One example takes the form of synchronicities (when words you are thinking about appear at the same time in songs, on the TV, on the computer, etc.). Having strong hunches that you hear over and over again and preoccupy your thoughts is another. In addition to these, I put my fingers on the computer keys when asking a question and start typing the letters that I hear. I have learned a great deal that way. The most important thing to remember is that the more you trust this voice, the louder it gets—and the more you use it, the more consistently you will hear it.

Dimension(s)

To better define and understand what a dimension is, we need to think of it as a point of perception rather than an actual place. For example, in the third dimension you are rooted in the physical world. You see yourself as a separate entity—there is me and there is you. You seek happiness outside and need things such as money, possessions, relationships, and status to feel fulfilled. In the fourth dimension, consciousness begins to awaken and you feel connected with others. The old ways of the third dimension seem antiquated. You still have comparison and judgment, but with more spiritual themes. When you enter the fifth dimension, it all changes. You follow your inner guidance. One's perception is more about unity consciousness—one for all and all for one. The ego evolves into a more loving mechanism. You begin to realize that what manifests in the outside world (negative and positive) is a result of what still exists in you. You no longer try to change the world, but rather begin to heal yourself and understand that love is the only true power.

Divine Feminine/ Divine Masculine

This is a dualistic belief that all things in the universe are interconnected, similar to the concept of yin and yang: there is a bit of masculine in the feminine and feminine in the masculine. Simply put, the divine feminine is the counterpart to the divine masculine; both together keep the universe in balance. These sacred polarities are compared to the heart and brain, the spirit and the earth, and/or the spirit and matter. These labels are simply poetic metaphors for the wholeness that you are. All of creation is simply the result of these two principles working together. The divine feminine qualities emphasize going inward—insight, nurturing, care, trust, patience, loyalty, love, honesty, understanding, empathy, compassion, forgiveness, healing, creativity, and receptivity. The sacred masculine is about exploring the outer world—action, achievement, doing, courage, independence, leadership, assertiveness, order, and strength. As we as a species approach a new dimensional "event horizon," everything we knew and embraced from the past will be redefined and restructured—including the role and separation of the divine feminine and divine masculine.

Dualism

If you believe there is good/bad, right/wrong, negative/positive, then you are embracing duality. We live in a system that identifies things such as up/down, right/left, and top/bottom. But as we move into different ways of thinking and perceiving, we will understand that the reality we currently accept to be true is more like a Band-Aid covering up the truth. Linear thinking will evolve into spherical thinking, and outdated labels and associations will fade away. Quantum physics will explain what we call coincidences and synchronicities and will open the door to the next chapter of human evolution.

Egregore

Mark Stavish has brought this word into the public consciousness with his book *Egregores: The Occult Entities That Watch Over Human Destiny,* published in 2018. An egregore is a thoughtform created by the collective thoughts of a distinct group of people (a family, a club, a political party, a church, or a country). It can be formed either intentionally or unintentionally and has the potential to become an autonomous entity with the power to influence. It can have a negative or positive influence depending on the energy and/or the type of thought of the group that summons it. You will see and experience egregores if you belong to any established groups. You are an independent entity—be careful not to give your power away. Check in with your heart regularly. If something doesn't feel right or resonate, maybe that group isn't for you.

Endorphin(s)

If you exercise regularly, you know the effect of an "endorphin high"—it helps put a bounce in your step and elevates whatever mood you are in. Endorphins are nature's pain and stress relievers. They are nicknamed the "happy hormones" because they make you feel really good. Endorphins, along with dopamine, oxytocin, and serotonin, create a compound that, when released into the body, helps you feel mentally and physically better. From them, physical pain is reduced and healing is enhanced. What is nice about endorphins is that the body makes them naturally (with some encouragement)—you don't need to take any pills. So—how do you get your brain to release these endorphins and give you this natural high? Some ways are eating a good piece of chocolate, great-tasting food (including spices), getting a massage, taking a hot bath, getting out the diffuser and enjoying aromatherapy, laughing like when you were a child, meditating, performing acts of kindness, and/or raising your pulse (perhaps dancing tonight?).

Energetic Field/Signature

If you bring the palms of your hands close together (not touching) and move them gently closer together and then farther apart very slowly a few times, you can sense something dense or spongy between them. The more you concentrate, the denser it becomes. You might even feel some tingling in your hands while doing this. You have just made conscious contact with your energy field (aka aura or energy signature). The human energy field is thought to be composed of a set of energy bands that graduate in color and frequency as they move outward from the physical body. Each of the bands or fields is part-nered with an energy center (chakra).

Everything on this planet (including the planet) has one. From the thoughts we construct to the physical, tangible creations in front of us, everything is energy. And this energy takes on who you are, what you think, believe, feel, manifest, and value. Just like you have created specific named accounts on social media, you have created a fingerprint energy signature of who you are and what you believe. Before you even open your mouth, sensitive people can "feel" and/or "read" you. Your energy signature is what communicates to others whether you are a positive or negative person and approachable or not. Energy is constantly moving and shifting, so who you are (and the account you have created) can be changed and renamed at any time.

Enlightenment

This word has been thrown around in every religion, time period, and spiritual circle for centuries. In the past, it has been defined as something that comes to you after you have worked hard for it—and followed very precise rules. These rules could deal with what you eat, how you breathe, where you live, and what you engage in or don't. All would agree that when you are enlightened (that is, when you see the Sun/son's light) you will be finished here in this dimension. You will be released from the wheel of karma and reincarnation and return to "Oneness" in the Universe. Although only a few special beings are reported to have attained this status (such as Buddha, Mohammed, Christ, and some monks here and there)—I know it is open to all who knock on its door. Enlightenment is put up on a pedestal as an unreachable quest. I believe, though, it is very accessible to us all. How you achieve it is very personal and individual. Some say you can achieve it through meditation, breathing, and pulling away from the material world. But if you believe you can walk the tightrope of illusion and truth and keep your balance, you can achieve it. •

Fleur-de-Lis

This small iconic symbol packs a big punch. Although most of us know this form from its use in popular culture and decoration (it appears on everything from wallpaper to clothing to depict luxury), it has a much more interesting and meaningful history. A fleur-de-lis is recognized as a stylized depiction of a lily flower (even though it looks more like an iris): three petals bound together in their center. But its roots grow deep into our history and stretch well into ancient Egypt. The flower shape grew out of something a bit more ominous. The shape of the flower echoes a winding snake and is considered to be an early prototype (Cleopatra was purportedly bitten by an asp). The fleur-de-lis also has predecessors in ancient Mesopotamia, Babylonia, Greece, and even Rome. The fleur-de-lis of Rome actually came to represent fidelity and unity among the people. In Christianity, it is easy to see why it is associated with the Virgin Mary because lilies are all about innocence, purity, and virtue. Most commonly, the fleur-de-lis is associated with French history because French monarchs adopted the symbol to tout that they were divine rulers appointed by God. The Boy Scouts of America took their logo from a fleur-de-lis found on a compass. It was chosen to symbolize that, like a compass, the boys are reliable and can always lead others home. Today, the fleur-de-lis pattern is desired for its association with being regal, classy, and a high-status figure.

Flower of Life

The Flower of Life is actually God's shorthand for life and the divine plan. This symbol is the source of all consciousness as we know it. The phrase *Flower of Life* doesn't stem from the flower pattern, but from the cycle of a fruit tree (from buds to fruit, to seeds, to new trees, etc.). It is a geometric symbol that typically has nineteen overlapping circles, forming a lovely, balanced, harmonic (symmetrical) design. It originates with one circle, and all other circles are built up around that. This symbol is said to be the basic template for everything in existence. And if you look hard enough, you will see many different hidden forms and patterns start to magically appear. We call these shapes sacred geometry—harmonic (whole). The Merkaba, Metatron's Cube, and Platonic solids originate from these sacred energetic structures. Inside these, the star tetrahedron, cube, octahedron, dodecahedron, and the icosahedron continue within these structures. How beautiful are the cycles of life—that they continue against all odds? Know that you are part of this miracle and are here to ensure its continuance.

Frequency Key/Doorway

Everything in this universe is made up of energy. Energy is made up of spinning and vibrating atoms that can act as particles or waves. The number of waves that pass a fixed point in time creates a frequency. These waves move, flow, and change all the time. A frequency key is an energy picked up by your body. Like the planet Earth, we all have a frequency key or resonance that we attune with. The planet's frequency key is 8 Hz (the Schumann resonance)—the electromagnetic "beat" of Earth. The Earth's aura, so to speak, is a giant spherical resonator, the cavity of which is filled with a weak electrically conductive medium. When your frequency aligns, attunes, or regulates with the planet's sound, you enter an energetic doorway into a personal spiritual consciousness. There you will feel brighter, clearer, and more harmonious. As the planet's vibrations shift and rise, we synchronize with these waves and shift too. Each of us resonates at a specific frequency. When I paint a spirit narrative commission for someone, they have to give me permission to connect with their personal frequency key to access imagery, verbal messages, and their Akashic Record.

Gaia

Gaia is another name for our home planet Earth. It is the symbol of all life, and in Greek mythology, Gaia was the great divine mother of all. It is this association that has us think of Gaia as Mother Nature. It does not merely represent the literal physical planet but also includes the forces, laws, and intelligence of nature. Many believe that Gaia is not just a rock floating in space but more like a spiritual entity or counterpart that cocreates with us. She is like a parent who aids, guides, and provides us with everything we need to thrive in this dimension. Gaia tries hard to take care of all her children and keep them balanced. Humans don't always make it easy for her!

Heart/Mind

Many believe that conscious awareness originates in the brain alone and that we think only with our brain. There is research that says this is not accurate. Even as far back as ancient Egypt, it was believed that the soul was part of the *ib,* or heart, and the heart, not the brain, was the seat of emotion, will, and intention. We do not give the heart its full credit; it does much more than we realize. Recent scientific research suggests that consciousness actually emerges from the brain and body acting together. Growing evidence suggests that the heart plays a particularly significant role in this process. Far more than a simple pump, as was once believed, scientists now recognize the heart as a highly complex system with its own functional "brain." It is a sophisticated sensory organ for receiving and processing information. The nervous system within the heart (or the "heart brain") enables it to learn, remember, and make functional decisions independent of the brain's cerebral cortex. There have been numerous experiments that show that the signals the heart continuously sends to the brain influence the function of higher brain centers involved in awareness, understanding, and emotional processing. The heart/mind has the important role of moving ideas into physical reality with love and compassion.

Imagination

If you ever solved a problem by visualizing it, you were using your imagination. Imagination is the internal camera that projects inside your third eye and is directly linked with Source, or infinite possibilities. Albert Einstein said, "Imagination is more important than knowledge. Knowledge is limited. Imagination encircles the world." And I would add to that, the universe. The word comes from the Latin verb *imaginari,* meaning "to picture oneself." It is also associated with the Greek word *phantasia,* meaning "imagination" or "appearance." Research does confirm that imagination is a neurological reality. It is much more powerful in our daily lives than previously thought. To take that concept further, without imagination, there would be no creativity, inventions, or progress of any sort.

Imprinting

Simply put, from the day you are born here on Earth, your senses collect information from your environment. This phenomenon is a preprogrammed drive stored in the body, mind, and—I believe—even in the soul. Birds and mammals (us) imprint on our parents as well as anything we are consistently exposed to when we are young. This process usually happens to the vulnerable— like newborns—but I feel it can happen at any age. Another definition of *imprinting* would be copying something until it is integrated and becomes automatic behavior. I use the term in a slightly different way. When someone or something in your life repeats information (whether accurate or not) until you believe it (as in school, the media, etc.), this is a form of imprinting. You are taught to trust these sources. This process works on us because we are, in reality, a very young and impressionable species. It is a form of brainwashing, brain-training, or entrainment. The force used on us is subtle but persistent, and one rarely knows when it is occurring. When you see life from a different perspective, you break the hypnotic "spell" you are under.

Intuition

Intuition is often associated with people who are able to feel and sense their world through an inner vision or a heightened sensory awareness. It has been used interchangeably with the terms *third eye, ESP,* or even *witchcraft*. The third eye or intuition takes place in an actual organ between our eyes; it is in this organ that our senses and mind collaborate as a larger, more powerful sensory organ. In practice, third eye intuition acts as a switch that activates higher states of consciousness and experiences of spiritual vision. It is a natural part of every person, but has been forgotten and therefore temporarily turned off. When reactivated or awakened, it guides us to new insights and understandings. It's the part of empathy where a person can touch and feel the emotions of others. If you can easily sense what others are feeling or thinking, then you are intuitive and found the voice and have wisdom of your heart.

Karma

Karma is the groove you create by repeating behaviors and choices starting when you are born. Karma is thought to be an ancient system built into and vibrating in your DNA. Many believe that karma continues from one lifetime to another. I do not. Karma is a system of belief we have bought into perpetrated by an outside force. Once you believe in it, you strengthen its power by doing things you think you are supposed to do or listening to what others tell you to do. It really doesn't have anything to do with reward and punishment. I use the word only because it is a popular concept, but I believe it is slowly shifting out of our reality as more people let it go. Karma only has power over you if you resonate with it. When you no longer believe in blame or victims, you will shift. In this new system, you will be taking control of your life and actions, deciding for yourself what your passion(s) will be and how you will use them.

Kundalini

Kundalini is a latent force that is part of the human organism. This Sanskrit word is all about awakening the sleeping energy in your spine—specifically located at the base of your spine. Kundalini is described as a "coiled snake" that is meant to be awakened. This process of uncoiling the snake—connecting us with divine energy—is called kundalini awakening. As kundalini energy rises, it's believed to help balance the chakras and contribute to your spiritual wellness. The dictionary says the history of kundalini practice comes from the lineage of raj yoga, one of the oldest forms of yoga mentioned in the sacred Vedic collection of texts known as the Upanishads and practiced in India since 500 BCE.

Light Body

The light body (aka astral, etheric, or Merkaba body) is called the chariot of the soul since it is believed to help us find our way back home to Source. The light body is in direct contact with your over-soul, or Divine Presence, and seems to be programmed with directions to our true home location—or what is commonly called "Ascension." We live in a matrix of light grids where everything around us is made up of photons energetically woven together. We are part of that structure. There are multiple layers of electromagnetic fields of energy that extend all around your physical body like an energy shield. As an artist, I see this body as a poetic jacket made of protective energy originating from the heart chakra.

Lightworker

Lightworker is a term used for people who feel that they are here at this time to help shift humanity into a higher level of consciousness. These sensitive souls help heal others through the use of their voice, words, or hands. They respect life, the environment, and each other. They want to see peace and harmony spread throughout the world, and they have a sense of urgency to make a positive difference in the world now.

Light Language

From my experience, light language comes from a connection with one's inner guides, such as angels, spirit guides, entities, and/or your family on the other side of the veil of knowledge. There are as many different light languages as there are languages on this planet—if not more. These languages can only be understood with intuition and heard with the heart. If you try too hard to understand and translate them with the egoic mind, the result will come out as incoherent sounds. All spoken languages are made up of sound vibrations that are projected outward and need a receiver to be heard and decoded. I would say that another term for light language would be *language of the heart.*

Looping

One form of looping is when you find your mind going in circles, repeating the same thought over and over again. It takes different strategies to stop this from happening once started. But I use the term more broadly and universally. I believe we are all looping through time and space, repeating ourselves over and over again—seamlessly moving from one life to another—totally unaware of the process. You can sense it sometimes (with what we call déjà vu) but never really grasp the truth of the situation. Some people use drugs, herbs, medicines, and/or meditation to try to break through the wall of forgetfulness and connect with the "truth," but for most, this wall is impenetrable. There have been a few—what I call "Energy Masters"—who have broken the code, so to speak, but most of us will live our lives unaware of our true situation.

Magical Thinking

This term is often used in reference to mental illness and New Age philosophies to describe a belief in something that doesn't exist or is inconceivable at the present time. But in truth, as we move through different densities/dimensions and our understanding of quantum physics progresses, what was once considered impossible will evolve and shift. What is going on now is similar to what was going on in the past when scientists and polymaths who were well ahead of their time were considered heretics or, even worse, mad. There are still forces working on controlling how much "truth" we can or should handle according to their agenda. That is why it is so important that you stay impartial and trust your inner "truth" more than what seems real in the outer world.

Matrix

A matrix is an artificial structure similar to a grid. The movie *The Matrix* has made the term part of popular culture, and I would be surprised if most people haven't heard of it. In the movie, people are trapped inside a simulated reality. It is a system of control that operates completely in the mind. In general, a matrix can be made up of anything. Since I believe everything is made of sound, and sound is vibration, and vibration is constructed of sacred geometric patterns, then we are indeed living in some sort of matrix. One way or the other, we are part of a world of hidden codes and mathematical formulas and must learn to navigate this matrix to do what we came here to do!

Med-Bed

Any good sci-fi movie has a med-bed lab as part of the scenery. *Star Trek* probably had the earliest, *Stargate* had an updated Egyptian sarcophagus that healed all human medical issues, and in *The Martian* Matt Damon had everything he needed to stitch up an intense, deep puncture wound on an isolated Mars base—and survive. If you think med-beds are science fiction, you would be wrong. Many different forms currently exist and are just starting to be discussed and acknowledged. This machine can heal human DNA in a way that is revolutionary. Only those with deep pockets could afford one now, so most of us would not have access to them for a while. But there are new options on the horizon, and it is only a matter of time before the medical system will have to change over to this new technology and begin a new age and world without pharmaceuticals.

Meditation

For most people, the word *meditation* conjures up the vision of a person sitting cross-legged with their eyes closed and fingers in a mudra (hand position). This is one form, but not the only one. The word *meditation* comes from the Latin *meditatus* and *medēri,* which means "to remedy." In the West, meditation has become synonymous with breathing and relaxation; people practice meditation to "destress." Most meditation focuses on one's breath and slows down the body's natural biorhythms. It enables us to move from higher-frequency brain waves to lower-frequency ones such as theta. It is in this state that the conscious mind gives way to the intuitive mind and we experience a calmness that helps heal the body.

Mindful

Most of our days are so busy that we tend to function on autopilot just to get through them. Being mindful means slowing down, turning up your senses, and becoming aware of each moment. When you are mindful, you are an observer, letting nothing pull you into its drama. In some ways, when you tune in to your mind, become an observer, and abandon your ego, you tap into what in the movies would be called superhuman abilities. The more mindful you are, the fewer dramas (accidents, misunderstandings, traumas, etc.) you have.

Mind-Meld

The most obvious definition of a *mind-meld* is that two minds merge into one. The concept originated on *Star Trek* with Spock—a Vulcan. Vulcans had the ability to merge their minds via their fingertip points with other humanoids, usually around the temples. This was done to extract the truth of a situation. I have been dreaming of minds merging between people since I was very young. Recently, I watched a series on Netflix where a husband and wife have cutting-edge technology implanted in each other's brains and know each other's thoughts all the time (she wasn't given a choice). That was a terrible idea!

Miracle

A miracle is a state of mind. When learned, limited belief systems are suspended and replaced by new templates of possibilities—what we thought we knew to be reality shifts. Miracles are normal phenomena being interpreted by outdated equipment, which is unable to define what is actually happening. Keep focusing on your heart/mind connection and believe that anything is possible.

Monkey Mind

If you have ever traveled to an exotic place and experienced the energy of monkeys hopping around trying to steal your banana, then you know what it is like to have a monkey mind. This is a continuous state where your thoughts are on fast-forward and you can't seem to slow them down. Eventually, it affects your everyday life. Sleep becomes challenging, and you can seem quite distracted. The Buddhists coined the term *monkey mind* and defined it as "unsettled, restless, confused, indecisive, or uncontrollable." The only way out of it is to face the monkey and let it know it is loved and safe. Breathe with it and slow everything down. Ultimately, your mind is in fear mode that has to be switched off. There are many ways to do this, such as meditation, exercise, or just good conversation with family or friends. Make a list of everything that needs to be done and slowly and steadily address them all. Usually, this condition is not life threatening—it is more annoying than anything else—but could cause health issues if not dealt with. It just takes time and love.

Morphic Resonance/Field

This is an energy that connects and organizes all living things with vibratory patterns. It is how we can have a collective unconscious—among other things. In the words of Rupert Sheldrake (the promoter/introducer of this term), "It enables memories to pass across both space and time from the past. The greater the similarity, the greater the influence of morphic resonance. What this means is that all self-organizing systems, such as molecules, crystals, cells, plants, animals, and animal societies, have a collective memory on which each individual draws and to which they contribute. In its most general sense, this hypothesis implies that the so-called laws of nature are more like habits" (from an interview by John Horgan, "Scientific Heretic Rupert Sheldrake on Morphic Fields, Psychic Dogs, and Other Mysteries," *Scientific American,* July 14, 2014). In other words, if one creature learns something, so do all the others. This makes things a lot easier—no?

Mystical

If you find yourself looking for answers about life in places other than established dogma or ordinary human knowledge, chances are you are a mystical person. You look for the divine through religion, the paranormal, metaphysical, or supernatural. The mystical is something that is mysterious and therefore not known. It is not under any current rules of science and therefore more likely to find some new system or phenomena previously undiscovered.

Myth

A myth is a story passed down over time from generation to generation. Most agree that there is a degree of truth in these stories—although a myth is commonly believed to be a fantasy. Since I believe we can't dream up what you don't already know, it is more likely that these stories have been labeled as myths so that the truth will not be known.

Oxytocin

Humans love to dissect everything. One of the latest discoveries is oxytocin. In the field of science, oxytocin has become a star. Just google it and see all the hits. Why? Because it all comes down to love! Oxytocin is a hormone secreted by the posterior lobe of the pituitary gland, a pea-sized structure at the base of the brain. It's sometimes known as the *cuddle hormone* or the *love hormone,* because it is released when people snuggle up or bond socially. It's a neuropeptide, a short-chain polypeptide that's used as a neurotransmitter, relaying a signal from one neuron to another.

This chemical is what gives humans the desire to take care of their young or protect a hurt animal. This hormone even plays a role in platonic relationships—promoting trust and generosity. In general, this is a positive chemical, but since it binds together those who are alike, it may explain what happens with egregores (which reinforces the group ideology by repelling anything that is different). Always remember to feel with your heart at the same time as you think with your head (and chemicals).

Paradise

The concept of a paradise that existed in the past where everything was beautiful, heavenly, and all our needs were met is actually a mistranslation. The biblical translation states that the human species lived on Earth in a gorgeous garden where love and innocence ruled—but then we sinned (we wanted knowledge and the truth) and were kicked out forever. In my research, I have come across another meaning of the word *paradise* from the Webster's Dictionary. *Paradise* means "an enclosure." The dictionary defines an *enclosure* as "an area that is sealed off with an artificial or natural barrier." I would say that it is more akin to a park, a prison, or even a zoo. For some reason, the authors of the Bible had a specific agenda and wanted to cover up the real story of our beginning. If you want to experience true paradise on Earth, see beauty everywhere and be grateful for everything—even one flower.

Pendulum

A pendulum is a tool used in dousing and divination. It is often made out of crystal (although it can be made out of anything heavy enough and symmetrically balanced) and hung from a chain or cord. It is a way of connecting with your intuition or, as some believe, your spirit guides or Higher Self. You can ask yes or no questions, and the pendulum will swing either back and forth or in clockwise or counterclockwise directions. You need to determine your yes and no before starting. Don't worry if you can't find a pendulum—you can use your own body. The human body acts like a musical instrument, with every organ, tissue, and bone in a constant state of vibration. It will respond to your thoughts. Just stand up straight and let yourself gently sway and feel yourself vibrating. Ask your question and see which direction your body moves—same as with the pendulum.

Psychic

Everyone has psychic powers to a certain degree, but like anything else, it depends how much you practice this skill. Someone who calls themselves a psychic medium has the mental ability to link with energy. When you think, your thoughts give off energy like a signal, and the psychic is able to receive that signal. You may willingly or unwillingly (or knowingly or unknowingly) allow someone to "read" your energy, but something is actually happening. I have seen someone document a psychic doing a session—it was recorded by a machine that apparently read energy and showed it on a screen in color based on heat signatures. The result was very interesting, showing both people being engulfed and linked together by energy. The same goes for those who have passed. They give off something in the physical realm that psychics can pick up. Everything one day will be explained by science.

Quantum Physics/Entanglement

To understand quantum physics, one has to stop thinking with a linear mind. This science doesn't fit nicely into present-day theorems. In this world, nothing is ever known for certain—we can only guess where something like an electron in an atom is located. Even Albert Einstein was stumped and called quantum entanglement "spooky action at a distance." Quantum entanglement explains, on some level, why we are all linked together and that what happens to one of us happens to us all. This phenomenon describes the strange quantum law that two subatomic particles are linked together no matter how far apart they are in space. Despite their distant locations in space, any change in one will affect the other in the same manner.

Ritual

Do you find yourself doing the same thing day after day, week after week, year after year without questioning why? Do you ever use the word *should* when performing certain activities? If so, chances are you have either personal or communal rituals. Rituals are usually associated with religious ceremonies but extend to our daily routines. They are neither good or bad—but they are typically performed automatically (done without thinking). The difference between a routine and a ritual is the attitude behind the action. It would benefit you to be aware of what routines and rituals you have and why you do them. A common ritual in religions is lighting a candle for someone who has passed away. Perhaps you were taught this in religious class when young and light one every Friday night. Well, when you perform this activity, are you really engaged in the process or are you doing it because you were told to and now it has just become a habit? Or do you do it because it is an important part of your day—you slow your life down and reflect on the beauty of the light and the person who has passed? Do you focus on love—of the person, self-love, and love of all things on the planet? If you have rituals in your life, be mindful of them and make them meaningful. When you do this, you send out balanced and loving vibrations into the cosmos and reap more benefits from it than you could ever imagine.

Sacred Geometry

Sacred geometry basically associates shapes with the divine. It is the key to all form in our existence—and has been described as the blueprint of creation. A series of shapes formed out of energy patterns shows how all life is organized. There are apparently codes (like in a computer program) that exist in our dimension that create everything we see around us and are why so many things repeat. The statement "as above, so below" is true because of sacred geometry. The most common shapes and/or symbols in sacred geometry are the triangle, square, circle, spiral, cross, Flower of Life, pyramid, Star of David, and Merkaba.

Shadow Side

The concept of a shadow side can be traced all the way back to ancient Egypt. In the book *The Nine Eyes of Light,* author Padma Aon Prakasha calls the shew (shadow) the Guardian to Source. He says, "The shew or shadow integrates your subconscious as well as the collective unconscious. It is a reflection of the world you create. We see into the deepest parts of ourselves and bring them back together again after being fragmented. To work with your shadow means connecting to the soul and the other bodies of light . . . As we explore, embrace, and integrate the shadow as a valuable part of ourselves, it opens up all our bodies to receive more light. We hold ourselves unconditionally and embrace ourselves as we are. The essence of the shadow is accessed when we go on the deepest journeys into the emptiness of our bodies and cells to bring back the gold of awakening and physical transformation. We see the devil and God at the same time. Then our soul can be free. The shadow wants to work with us, to be included. Once it is harnessed, included, and listened to, it has a voice that actually guards, protects, and aligns the soul to Source."

Shaman

The term *shaman* comes from the Manchu-Tungus word *šaman* and literally means "one who knows." Traditionally, shamans were part of indigenous or aboriginal societies and were healers, advisors, and keepers of the cultural traditions. They were either born with a special birthmark, veil, or somehow identified as different from all others in the group. They trained for the position early on in their lives and often took journeys into "other worlds" to gain knowledge or to protect others. They usually did not live as long as the ones they served. In the modern world, the term is used more loosely—it represents someone who has studied some particular interest like ayahuasca or drumming.

Shapeshifter

Shapeshifting refers to the ability that a humanoid being possesses to change in form, especially from human to animal or a change in appearance from one person to another. I actually experienced hearing one when I slept out in the woods at a sacred Native American site in New York called Hawk Rock. There were unnatural sounds—of a human shifting to an animal(s)—and back again. But symbolically, I would define a shapeshifter as the ability to dramatically alter who you are (your personality and/or your physical look—for specific reasons) and then return to your old self.

Soul

Your soul is that part of yourself that is pure energy; it is eternal. Souls hold on to aspects of your personality from one life to another. In the past, souls were subject to karma, but this is now shifting. Your soul is yours and yours alone. No one else has permission to use or control it!

Source

I use the word *Source* in place of the word *God* or *the infinite.* It refers to a place where all healing and creative ideas originate. It means universal energy; it is the power and force behind all that exists today on the planet. Source is not a physical place but a consciousness one can tap into. Whenever this word appears, you may substitute whatever term you associate with it.

Spherical Thinking

I thought up this term years ago only to find that it exists in quantum physics—of course! It is a completely different way of perceiving and explaining local phenomena. In the past, you would follow a logical, linear path to achieve your goals. Nothing else would matter or be important except for what you think you need to do. You would be oblivious to any signs or assistance that would contradict these beliefs—in fact, you might blame others and complain that they are not assisting you. Spherical thinking brings in new possibilities and ways to achieve your goals—usually considered "outside the box." This help comes from inside of you—it could be your Higher Self or what others call intuition.

But since you have not been trained to understand this guidance, you ignore it. You know you have tapped into spherical thinking when your path gets easier and you seem happier. Past and future don't fit into the equation, and only what is going on right now in the present defines success.

Spiritual Surgery

There are people who perform literal energetic surgery on people (like John of God), but I am using this term symbolically. Many are here at this time to help others be able to handle the new frequencies that are flooding our dimension. Some of us are naturally adapting and are doing just fine, while others are having a harder time of it. Those who choose to help others literally change who they are, what they think, and/or what they do—are performing a type of divine molecular do-over—or what I call spiritual surgery.

Squaring the Circle

Squaring the circle is a problem in geometry first proposed in Greek mathematics. It is the challenge of constructing a square with the area of a circle by using only a finite number of steps with a compass and straightedge. The author of the article on Wikipedia says that despite the proof that it is impossible, attempts to square the circle have been common in "pseudomathematics"—the work of mathematical cranks. Well, one of those cranks was Leonardo da Vinci, who was quite obsessed with this concept when he created his Vitruvian Man drawing. Although he didn't succeed in this image, he still tried. And he tried many more times. The expression *squaring the circle* has become a metaphor for trying to do something that is impossible. But as we all know, what people thought impossible a hundred years ago is now possible. And what current scientists and skeptics think is impossible will one day be the norm.

Stargate

The original concept of a stargate came from the movie *Stargate.* In the movie, a stargate is an Einstein–Rosen bridge portal device within the universe that allows practical, rapid travel between two distant locations. The characters in the movie could visit alien planets without the need for spaceships or any other type of technology. The device allowed for near-instantaneous travel across both interstellar and extragalactic distances. I believe we have "stargates," or portals to other times and places on and off the planet. They are used by beings who have the knowledge of how to manipulate time and space. Symbolically, I use the term as a way of accessing and experiencing new technologies and gaining a new perspective on life as we know it.

Supernatural

The term *supernatural* will eventually be considered archaic since nothing is beyond or greater than the natural truth. Currently, the term is used as something that doesn't fit into current expected belief patterns—specifically relating to God, a god, or a spirit. It departs from what is usual or normal—appearing to transcend the laws of nature. But as we evolve into fifth or higher dimensional beings, what we know as normal will change and the word will no longer be used.

Synchronicity

Like the term implies, *synchronicity* deals with events that synchronize together at the same time or rate. They happen all the time to most people, but few take notice. It usually involves thinking of something and having it happen (like a call from a long-lost friend) or hearing numbers and words as you read them. They happen all the time with the oracle decks I made and use with people (someone just contacted me about pulling the zebra card from the *Animal Love* deck—while she was wearing a black and white–striped dress). Synchronicity happens so often to me that I don't even use that word anymore—it's just a natural part of my consciousness and life. I have found, though, that these events are increasing, and people are finally beginning to acknowledge them and ask questions.

Telephathy/Telepathic

Telepathy is part of what is called psi. This is a neutral term for a group of paranormal behaviors, including extrasensory perception, precognition, and psychokinesis. It is from the Greek *psi,* the twenty-third letter of the Greek alphabet, and from the Greek *psyche,* "mind, soul." It is when one person sends out thoughts and feelings and another person receives them. Although this might sound like science fiction, it is far from it. Today, there are experiments being done that show that telepathy can be measured, even over the internet! Many of us do not need scientific proof, though; we know it happens all the time.

Timeline

The short definition of the term *timeline* in 3D is that time flows in a predictable progression of past, present, and future. That proposed movement creates a line in time that leads us to our next event. I love Alan Lew's take on what a timeline is. He states:

> Time does not exist. The past, present, and future all occur in the present moment point (the Now). You never directly experience the past or the future. You remember (or imagine) your past and you guess (or imagine) your probable futures. You only experience the present "Now." But when you are in the "Now," you do not experience time at all, nor do you have any thoughts. You transcend both . . . Your present moment "Now" is always the strongest point of your creative power. It is where you create your past, present, and probable futures. Another way to look at this is that each "Now" is a snapshot of a parallel reality. As you move from one "Now" to the next, you create and experience the flowing river of "time." As you choose the next parallel reality (or next "now") to experience, you create your individual and collective timelines . . . Each person chooses their ascension timeline, which forms their personal universe. You vibrationally co-create a shared universe with others.*

*"Explainer: 'Time' and 'Timelines'—What They Are and How To Use Them," Alan Lew (Medium website: New Earth Consciousness, 2021).

So, a timeline is a subjective journey we all choose to take. It can change at any point if you decide that the current direction isn't to your liking. You are free to choose your destiny—it doesn't choose you.

Time Travel

If you watch enough sci-fi movies, it would seem that time travel is possible—at least in the human imagination. And if what you put your attention to manifests (quantum law), then indeed, time travel is possible. From what I have been reading and watching, it appears that there have always been time travel capabilities and time travelers. It is something our government has known of and been researching—and they even advertised for time travelers years ago (and found one!). Since nothing is as it seems, then I would have to postulate that the concept of time is an illusion, a construct made up (as in a computer program), and that we, and other life-forms, have been visiting ourselves from the future all along. Maybe it is simpler than it seems. When we close our eyes and go deep into our imaginations (or when we dream), where do we go?

Transformation

The term *transformation* is used a great deal. In general, it is defined as one thing or form changing into some other form. The word appears in the midfourteenth-century Old French from Latin *transformare*—meaning "change the form of, change the shape, metamorphose." *Trans* means "across, beyond," and *formare* means "to form." The New Age, spiritual, or metaphysical version of transformation refers not so much to physical change but to the evolution of the soul. I like how Ken Wilber sees human transformation. He tells us to "Grow Up by moving through the early stages of emotional maturing; Clean Up by doing shadow-up; Wake Up by doing spiritual practice; and Show Up by serving humanity in the world."

Trichroism

When three colors dance, shift, and change in a crystal, that crystal displays trichroism. The word comes from the Greek *trikhroos,* meaning "three-colored," from *tri-* ("three") and *khrōma,* meaning "color." The technical definition of *trichroism* is a stone that displays biaxial crystals that cause a perceptible difference in color when viewed along three different axes. Tanzanite (along with iolite, andalucite, and emerald) is one of the few gemstones that display this characteristic. These eye-catching stones are sensitive to the light source they are viewed under, so the same stone can appear very different in varying circumstances.

Unconditional Love

Unconditional love is a popular term and most think they know what it is (love with no strings attached). But knowing something and integrating it are two different things. We need to embrace this concept if we are going to be mature beings in this multiverse. We are programmed from birth with different needs and exposed to the societal whims of the time. Unconditional love means that no matter what the circumstances are in life, you know how to love: no judgments, no prejudices. You love yourself, your family, your friends, you treat all living things with respect (nature, animals, plants, the planet, the universe, etc.). You will know you have integrated unconditional love when you smile and laugh a lot—and your heart sings with joy every day of your life. It doesn't mean you don't feel sadness; you do—but you move past it easily and lovingly. Nothing can throw you off balance when you are in this state; after all, embracing unconditional love opens the door to the fifth dimension. All you have to do is walk in.

ABOUT THE AUTHOR

Nadine Gordon-Taylor has had the ability to sense and experience other beings since childhood. She maintains the Third Eye Arts Studio and Gallery in the city of Peekskill, New York. There she sells her art and gives readings with her oracle decks. Born in Queens, New York, she studied at the Art Students League while attending high school and college. She earned a BA with a concentration in printmaking and art history at Hunter College and her MFA in painting from Long Island University. Her EdD in art education is from Columbia University. She has studied comparative religion and alternative healing modalities to help inform her art.

Before embarking on her journey as an intuitive artist and working with universal and intuitive symbols, Nadine focused on photorealist drawing and painting of her shadow—integrating, embracing, and honoring her dark side. She has taught publicly and privately for more than thirty years and has lectured and given workshops across the country. Her drawings, prints, and paintings have been exhibited and are in collections around the world.

PURCHASING AN IMAGE
FROM THE DECK

All the images in the *Crystal Clear Oracle* are available for purchase. For more information, please visit

www.thethirdeyestudio.com

You can also contact Nadine via email at

ngtartist@gmail.com

You can follow her on Facebook at Third Eye Arts Studio and Gallery, on Instagram at The_Third_Eye_Studio, and TikTok at Thirdeyearts.

Thank you for purchasing
Crystal Clear Oracle

We are all on the hero's journey, waking up from a form of spiritual amnesia. Have patience with yourself and others. Be conscious of your mission and fight with the most powerful weapon you possess—your heart! You are all my eternal partners and heroes. Never forget the power you hold with just your mind and thoughts. You are creative, brilliant, and, most importantly, resilient beings! Add to that your unwavering determination, and together we will manifest Heaven on Earth!